Teshuvah

Inspiration, Stories & Practical Advice

REBBETZIN S. FELDBRAND

Copyright 2008 by S. Feldbrand
First edition - First impression / July 2008
Published by Lishmoa Lilmod U'Lelamed

ALL RIGHTS RESERVED

Distributed by:

Israel Book Shop
501 Prospect Street
Lakewood, NJ 08701
Tel: (732) 901-3009
Fax: (732) 901-4012
e-mail: info@israelbookshoppublications.com

ISBN: 978-1-60091-069-2

Printed in Canada.

Jacket design and typesetting: Zippy Thumim

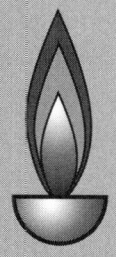

לעילוי נשמת אבי ומורי
ר׳ יהושע אלי׳ בן ר׳ חיים שאול גראסמאן ע״ה
אשר הרבה פעל בהדפסת והפצת ספרים
על טהרת הקדש, ספר זה מוקדש לנשמתו
הטהורה שתעלה מעלה מעלה בגן עדן.

וגם לעילוי נשמת מורי וחמי
ר׳ חיים יהודה בן ר׳ יצחק מאיר ע״ה
דוגמא של עין טובה ורוח נמוכה
ונפש שפלה, שישתשע בנחלי אוהבי יש.

וגם לעילוי כל הנשמות שאין להם מליץ יושר.
תנצב״ה

Rabbi P. Hirschprung
230 Querbes
Montreal, Quebec
Tel. 514-276-9886

I was shown a book in English by Rebbetzin Feldbrand, relating to the topic of *tefillah*. She has assembled material which is certain to inspire its readers to heightened worship of Hashem, so that they are more acutely aware before Whom they stand in prayer. The various concepts on the power and importance of *tefillah* are sure to make prayers more meaningful for all. May Hashem accept our prayers for general and particular salvation. We should all merit to behold the Bais Hamikdash in its glory, in compassion, speedily in our days.

Translation of Rabbi Hirschprung, chief rabbi of Montreal's, *zt"l,* approbation to a previous sefer, *Towards Meaningful Prayer*, by Reb. S. Feldbrand.

Table of Contents

Acknowledgements xiii
Preface xvii
Introduction: The Power of Teshuvah 1
1   Hashem Awaits our Teshuvah 9
2   The Nature of Sin 15
3   The Principle of Teshuvah 20
4   Definitions of Teshuvah 27
5   The Dynamics of Teshuvah 33
6   The Need to Repent 41
7   The Teshuvah Process 44
8   When to Repent 51
9   Suffering and Teshuvah 62
10 *Cheshbon Ha'nefesh* 66
11 Prompt Repentance 76
12 Beginning the Teshuvah Process 86
13 Change Must Be Gradual 93
14 The Four Components of Teshuvah: Regret 98
15 The Four Components of Teshuvah:
    Abandonment of Sin 110

16	The Four Components of Teshuvah: Confession and Asking for Forgiveness	113
17	The Four Components of Teshuvah: Resolution Not to Repeat	122
18	Shame	126
19	Teshuvah for Bad *Middos*	132
20	Humility as an Aid to Teshuvah	136
21	The Depths of Heavenly Judgment	141
22	Teshuvah out of Fear	147
23	Teshuvah out of Love	154
24	A Week of Repentance	157
25	Shofar and Repentance	159
26	Everyone is Urged to Return	171
27	The Greatness of a *Baal Teshuvah*	176
28	No Excuses	185
29	Hashem Helps	190
30	Two Types of Purification	194
31	The Significance of Elul	202
32	Asking Others for Forgiveness	211
33	Shortcuts to Teshuvah	225
34	The Study of *Mussar* and Teshuvah	229
35	Repeating the Teshuvah Process Again and Again	234
36	The *Yetzer Hara*'s Deterrent to Teshuvah	241
37	Sincere Teshuvah	249
38	Teshuvah and Redemption	254
39	Teshuvah and *Simchah*	259
40	Charity and Repentance	269
41	Teshuvah and Shabbos	272
42	Collective Teshuvah	274

43	Teshuvah in *Tanach*	282
44	Barriers to Repentance	290
	Afterword	307

Acknowledgements

These words are a modest attempt to acknowledge a debt to numerous *baalei teshuvah* who have enriched my life in so many ways. My journey into the world of *kiruv* began some twenty-eight years ago when Rabbi Dovid Din, *z"l*, stood in our dining room, like a prophet of old, admonishing my husband and me that the *frum* community would be held responsible for not reaching out to assimilated Jews.

Rising to the challenge, we took our first tenuous steps into this holy enterprise. I'll never forget our first guest, a music aficionado who went on and on about the death of John Lennon. My husband whispered to me in Yiddish, "*Ver is das*? (Who is that?)" "*A goyishe zinger* (a non-Jewish singer)," I replied. But music is an international language with the power to navigate even the cultural gap between a Beatles fan and a *chassidishe* couple.

I cannot say who benefited more. Was it those whose hands I held as they navigated the road of return? Or did *I* benefit more, as I underwent the teshuvah process with the vibrancy and sparkle of a neophyte? To cite only one example that stands out in my mind: I first studied *Hilchos Teshuvah* of the Rambam about twenty-five years ago with a Brazilian *baalas teshuvah*. I greatly admired her. Her insights honed my sensitivities to the manifest possibilities in *avodas Hashem*.

Later encounters with newcomers to Yiddishkeit always left me the wiser, with new resources for my own growth. The dividends continue to accrue through former students who are now in *kiruv* themselves. Their activities are a constant source of joy in my life.

High up on the list of women I most admire are many *baalos teshuvah* who passed my summer camp's exit on their way to the Woodstock music festival in 1969. Who could have imagined then that the young people contributing to a horrific traffic jam that *Erev Shabbos* would one day benefit *Klal Yisrael* in such an astonishing way. The writing and lectures of those returneees are today some of our most stimulating reading and listening. We cannot quantify our benefits, both material and cosmic, from the countless sparks these spiritual giants generated as they journeyed upwards.

The result of their teshuvah was that my own teshuvah and that of so many others became so much more meaningful. For that I will be eternally grateful. This *sefer* is a tiny symbol of that *hakaras ha'tov*.

As always, my husband, Mayer, has lent his extensive knowledge to this endeavor. May Hashem enable him to continue being *marbitz Torah be'rabbim*. May we merit continued *nachas de'kedushah* from our children and grandchildren.

Acknowledgements

I would like to thank my friend Shayna Elka Falk for reviewing this manuscript and making many valuable suggestions. May Hashem repay her in kind for her generosity of spirit.

Rabbi Moshe Kaufman and his staff at Israel Book Shop have been extremely helpful, every step of the way, and I thank them. Many thanks to Yocheved Krems for editing and proofreading the manuscript, and Zippy Thumim for her skilled design and layout. May they be blessed with *hatzlochah* in all their endeavors.

Preface

This *sefer* is best studied one section at a time. Rav Shlomo Wolbe writes that teshuvah is a gradual process (*Alei Shor,* vol. 2, pg. 438). It is extremely vital not to proceed too quickly. The teshuvah process can be compared to climbing to the top floor of a high building. Walking nonstop is debilitating. The way to succeed is at a slow and steady pace. On the other hand, if we stop in the middle, we may give up. The most important thing to remember is: never become discouraged; never give in to despair.

Rosh Ha'shanah had arrived, and Mayer, a seventeen-year-old talmid of Rav Shimshon Pincus, was disheartened. Rav Pincus's inspiring shmuessen (Torah lectures) had made a distinct impression on Mayer. He had made commitments and resolutions to improve in his yiras Shamayim, davening, and learning. However, although he worked very hard to keep these commitments and resolutions, he felt that he had not progressed sufficiently to present himself to Hashem for the impending Judgment. As a result, he felt like a complete failure.

On Rosh Ha'shanah morning, Rav Pincus stepped outside the shul for a moment and spotted Mayer in the corner of the hallway, sitting on a low chair with his head between his knees. Rav Pincus, with warmth and caring, approached and placed his hand on Mayer's shoulder, and asked him why he seemed so sad.

Mayer looked up into his rebbi's eyes and poured out his frustration. He told him how hard he had tried during this past month to improve, but with no success. He had pledged that this Rosh Ha'shanah would be different, but it wasn't. Mayer cried bitterly and hung his head in shame, perceiving himself as a total failure.

Rav Pincus sat down next to the boy and related the following incident:

"During the Yom Kippur War, I was sitting in the emergency room in Shaarei Zedek waiting for one of my children to be seen by a doctor for a cut that apparently needed stitches. Suddenly, I noticed a commotion taking place. Many doctors had converged in front of the emergency room doors and appeared to be discussing an important matter.

"I asked what was going on and was told that a wounded soldier had arrived at the hospital with a bullet lodged in his leg that needed to be taken out. The doctor had removed the bullet, and told the soldier, who had been awake during the entire procedure, that he was free to go home. The young man, no older than nineteen, painfully struggled to slide off the operating table. Beads of sweat formed on his forehead. He looked curiously at the doctor.

" 'Home? You think I'm heading home? True, I was shot, but there's a war raging out there! My fellow soldiers need me back on the battlefield.' The brave young man hobbled out of the room and headed back toward the front lines."

As Rav Pincus concluded this story he looked into Mayer's eyes and said, "Mayer, I'm not going to try to convince you that you have not stumbled. But just because you've fallen does not mean you can't get back up. Losing a battle does not mean that you've lost the war. We're fighting a war there in shul today, and I don't want to head back into shul without you. We need you to fight alongside the rest of us!"

A shy smile formed on Mayer's face and he thanked his *rebbi* for the warm words of encouragement. With Rav Pincus's arm around Mayer's shoulder, the two walked together back into shul to continue to "fight" side by side.

Purposeful, steady, and consistent in the pursuit of teshuvah, and with a large dose of *siyata de'Shamaya*, we are sure to succeed. It is my hope that this *sefer* can play an important role in making us all worthy of the exalted title "*Baal Teshuvah*" — Master of Teshuvah.

An American once visited the Brisker Rav in Yerushalayim. "What is your occupation?" the Rav asked.

"I am a lawyer," replied the man.

Minutes later, the Rav again asked, "What is your occupation?"

"I am a lawyer," the man again replied.

"That is not how a Jew answers such a question!" the Rav told him. "How did the prophet Yonah answer it?" When his ship was beset by a storm, the sailors determined that Yonah was the cause. They asked him his trade and he answered, "Ivri anochi! [I am a Hebrew!] And I fear Hashem the G-d of the Heavens."

"That," said the Rav, "is every Jew's main occupation! Being a lawyer, real estate broker, accountant — is merely how he earns his living!"

We are all striving to increase our fear of Heaven and to submit ourselves to Hashem's will. Teshuvah is the force that enables us to constantly move to higher ground. May we merit to access to the power of that force. May it take us to the ever-greater level of closeness to Hashem, and may this bring *Moshiach*, speedily in our days.

S. Feldbrand
Brooklyn NY
June 2008

Introduction
The Power of Teshuvah

The voice that emanates from Mt. Sinai repeatedly calls out to each of us to repent for our sins. As long as we live, repentance is always a possibility. No matter now much wrong a person has done, Hashem will respond with boundless compassion. As long as we live, the gates of teshuvah are never closed (*Devarim Rabbah* 20:7). There is no hindrance or obstacle that stands in the way of a strong resolution to repent.

Before Hashem created the laws of nature, a principle even more fundamental and more exalted was proclaimed: that change — teshuvah — is possible. Teshuvah is one of the greatest kindnesses Hashem has granted us. With teshuvah we can alter reality, after the fact.

Teshuvah regenerates a person both physically and spiritually, lengthening a person's life. Teshuvah returns vitality to his malnourished limbs restoring a person's health (see *Yoma* 86). People will waste so much money and effort to heal themselves. They should invest even more time and effort in repentance. When a person repents, he is taken back to a previous chapter in his life, before he was ill, and in many instances his illness disappears (Maharal, *Nesiv Ha'teshuvah* 2).

> ### Inspiration
>
> Imagine a person standing before the Heavenly Court viewing the story of his life. All the sins he committed, all the mindless activities are on display. Of course the Court decides that he is guilty and he cries out, "Woe is me for the evil I committed and the life I wasted!" Imagine that at this point he was allowed to return to this world and repent. He wouldn't waste one minute! All other activities would be ignored as he scrambled to do teshuvah and repair all the damage he had brought about during the course of his life. Is it necessary for a person to die first to understand how important it is to throw himself into repentance?
>
> (*Mussar Yesamach Lev*, pg. 22)

Through teshuvah, a person's transgressions are forgiven and the blemish they inflicted on the transgressor's soul is wiped away (*Shaarei Teshuvah* 1:1). Teshuvah redefines the past, transforming the transgression from a break in our relationship with Hashem into an agent of even deeper connection and ultimately into veritable virtues. Teshuvah raises the *baal teshuvah* to a level from which "even the perfectly righteous cannot stand" (*Berachos* 34a).

> ### INSPIRATION
>
> Yesterday he was a sinner, hated and despised by Hashem, as it says: "Your sins form a barrier between you and your G-d. Even if you daven a lot, I shall not listen!" In that despicable state he had to deal with all sorts of trials sent his way to induce him to stop, reflect, and return. Today (after repenting) he is loved and cherished so much that his prayer is promptly answered. As it says, "And it shall be that before they even pray I shall answer" (see *Hilchos Teshuvah* of the Rambam).

The process of teshuvah enables us to see ourselves and our life with clarity and to recreate ourselves and watch the defects disappear. A restructured soul fashioned out of teshuvah from love will revolutionize a person's outlook and conduct. (*Hegyonos*) To achieve this goal, we must pull together all the positive forces within us. All good character traits must be mustered to produce proper teshuvah. Once we have gathered together all our internal forces, we must resolutely seek out external allies such as *seforim* on teshuvah, a teacher of *mussar*, and like-minded friends so that together we will be able to fashion a frontal offensive to pin down the *yetzer hara* and do proper teshuvah. (Adapted from the introduction to *Yesodei Ha'daas* by Rabbi Moshe Rosenstein)

In our own days we see clearly how awesome is the power of teshuvah. Contemporary events demonstrate that there is absolutely nothing that stands in the way of teshuvah. People who were so far away from Yiddishkeit are now vibrant members of our community. People who fought against our religion are now studying Torah full time. They are embracing the option of altering reality after the fact, removing their burdensome past and opening the door to a new and meaningful future.

All uninspired prayers that never ascended to Heaven are elevated when a person does teshuvah (Rav Yissachar Dov of Belz). Teshuvah breaks through the strongest barriers of iron and annuls all evil decrees (*Rosh Ha'shanah* 17; *Zohar Ha'kodesh* 2:106). The two guardian angels that abandon the sinner when he transgresses are restored after he repents (*Zohar, Mishpatim*). All uninspired prayers that never ascended to heaven are elevated when a person does teshuvah (Rav Yissachar Dov of Belz). Even a person who considers doing teshuvah but dies before he can reform himself will eventually rise from *Gehinnom*.

There is no sin that cannot be mended and remedied by teshuvah.

> *It was a glorious wedding. The* simchah *resonated from wall to wall, bouncing off the participants onto the* chassan *and* kallah*, and back. The joyous celebration began at the reception and reached its apex during the dancing. Finally it was the father of the* chassan's *turn to dance with his son. He removed his jacket and placed it on his chair. All eyes were on father and son as they warmly embraced and began twirling in time with the music. At long last, depleted, the father dropped his arms and returned to his seat. Instinctively he reached inside the pocket of his*

jacket. Anyone observing him would have noticed that his face suddenly turned deathly pale. The $10,000 he had brought for some of the evening's expenses was gone. It was difficult to restrain himself from calling out and alerting the police, but he could not bring himself to ruin the simchah. *It had cost so much. So it would cost another $10,000.*

The wedding and sheva berachos *passed. When the video of the wedding was ready, the two sets of parents sat down to replay the* simchah. *They saw the* chuppah, *the meal, and finally the dancing. The father of the* chassan *could be seen placing his jacket on the chair as he walked to dance with his son. Moments later the camera panned the hall and the father of the* kallah *could be seen placing his hand into the* chassan's *father's jacket pocket and removing an envelope.*

The lights were immediately turned on and everyone turned to look at the father of the kallah.

This story really happened. Try to put yourself in the shoes of that man. His theft was exposed. Consider for a moment his humiliation. What would he give to erase that small segment from the film and to delete that thirty-second episode? Let us take this scenario a step further. How much would we give to erase some deeds we have perpetrated, so that they will not appear in the final viewing of our life. When we do teshuvah, this is exactly what happens. We regret the deed and Hashem proceeds to erase it. (*Maayan Ha'moed*, pg. 93–95)

> ### Food For Thought
> So great is the power of teshuvah that when a person determines to do teshuvah, he rises immediately to the highest Heaven, to the very presence of the Throne of Glory.
>
> (*Pesikta Rabbasi* 44)

When Reb Boruch Ber of Kamenitz's father took ill, he sat at his father's bedside for countless days and nights. His students, fearful for his health, insisted that they could take over. He finally agreed to leave his father's bedside a few hours a day.

Shortly thereafter his father died. Reb Boruch Ber was hounded by the concern that he had not properly honored his father. The distress so devastated him that he had to stop giving his regular Torah lectures. He took advantage of a meeting of prominent rabbis in Vilna to pour out his heart to the Chofetz Chaim. The Chofetz Chaim spoke to him at length about the power of repentance. He stressed that teshuvah not only atones for the sin, but transforms the baal teshuvah *to a different person entirely. That new entity no longer has a connection to the past one. Reb Boruch Ber later said, "The Chofetz Chaim revived my spirit."*

(*Ha'rav Domeh Le'malach*, pg. 310–311)

Food For Thought

Rabbi Levi said, "Great is teshuvah, for it enables a person to reach the throne of G-d." As it says, "Return, O Israel, to the L-rd your G-d' [*Hoshea* 14:2]" (*Yoma* 86a). The principle is: No matter how far a person has distanced himself from G-d by his previous behavior, it is possible for him to return, depending on his effort, all the way to great closeness to his Creator. Teshuvah can sometimes work better than prayer because prayer's reception is dependant on merit, and interference may prevent it from reaching the Throne of Glory. (Maharsha, *Yoma* 86)

Rabbi Yochanan said, "Great is teshuvah, for it causes a person's verdict to be torn up" (*Rosh Ha'shanah* 17b). We are enjoined to do teshuvah as long as we have the strength, as long as the candle burns — until a person's death, there is no such thing as an irrevocable verdict. No matter how bad a person's behavior was, it is possible for him to have his Heavenly Verdict revoked. When we repent and seek forgiveness, our Father's compassion will assert itself. (*Yalkut Koheles* 979)

Whoever does teshuvah is regarded as if he had gone up to Yerushalayim, built the Sanctuary, built the Altar, and offered all the sacrifices prescribed in the Torah (*Vayikra Rabbah*).

Teshuvah, even when a person has sunk to the depths, can be immediate. In the span of one instant a *baal teshuvah* draws close to the Holy One, blessed be He, more so than the perfectly righteous, who draw near over the span of many years!

May Hashem help us do teshuvah properly so that we fulfill the words of "*Shuva Yisroel ad Hashem Elokecha*" [*Hoshea* 14]. We are assured that the Jewish People will repent sooner or later. Let us pray that it will be truly soon. We will then merit seeing the fulfillment of Hashem's pledge to the Jewish people, "A redeemer shall come to Tzion and to those of Yaakov who repent from willful sin" (*Yeshaya* 59:20).

Hashem Awaits Our Teshuvah

The most detailed description of the process of abandoning sin and repentance is found in the following passage in the Torah: "And it will be, when all these things come upon you, the blessing and the curse that I have placed before you — and you will [finally] take it to heart, among all the nations where G-d has dispersed you. You will return to Hashem your G-d, and you will listen to His voice ... you and your children with all your heart and all your soul. Then Hashem your G-d will return you from your exile, and have mercy on you; He will gather you in from all the peoples to which Hashem your G-d, has scattered you ... Hashem your G- d, will circumcise yours heart, and that of your children, to love Hashem your G-d will all your heart and with all your soul" (*Devarim* 30:1–6).

Some people have a custom of reading this section, known as *Parshas Ha'teshuvah*, daily, accompanied by a special prayer that Hashem help us to achieve a degree of *teshuvah shleimah* — complete repentance.

The beginning of the section implies that teshuvah is a process that must be undertaken *by us*. After undergoing sufficient punishment for our sins, we will realize that the blame lies within: "... and you will return to Hashem your G-d and listen to His voice ..." But later in the section, the Torah speaks about Hashem "circumcising our heart," implying that it is not really we who return to Hashem, but rather He Who removes the spiritual impediments preventing us from approaching Him. If Hashem, so to speak, must "circumcise our hearts," then what have we really accomplished?

Earlier in *Devarim* (4:25–29) the Torah also describes the teshuvah process: "When you ... will do evil in the eyes of Hashem your G-d, and anger Him. I appoint Heaven and Earth this day to bear witness against you — you will surely perish quickly from the Land ... Hashem will scatter you among the peoples ... From there you will seek Hashem your G-d, and you will find Him, if you search for Him with all your heart and all your soul."

Once again, we have man initiating teshuvah, but here there is no mention of Hashem "circumcising our hearts," perhaps implying that the entire process depends on us. However, the Torah describes the culmination of teshuvah as "finding Hashem." The term "to find" implies something that one has come across quite by chance without effort. Wouldn't it have been more appropriate to state that one will "attain" or "achieve" a certain level of teshuvah, as opposed to "finding" it?

In both sections the Torah expresses how teshuvah involves searching "with all one's heart and with all one's soul." In the first passage, the wording is used twice, once describing our teshuvah, and once when describing the stage after Hashem has circumcised our hearts: "Hashem, your G-d, will circumcise your heart, and that of your children, to love Hashem your G-d will all your heart and with all your soul." It seems unnecessary for the Torah to add these final words. Hashem is perfect, and so are all of His actions. If He circumcises our hearts and draws us close, obviously there will be an aspect of perfection in this, and we will serve Him with all our hearts and souls. Such words are only necessary when describing the requirement of teshuvah initiated by us.

The Yismach Moshe explains that teshuvah is a process begun, but not completed, by us. Hashem doesn't expect us to ever reach the level of complete teshuvah. He just tests us, again and again, to see how seriously we mean it, and if we're going to give up when the going gets tough. It's not a question of how far we can go, but how long we can persevere, and whether our determination to change can stand firm even in the face of trials and difficulties. In the Yismach Moshe's words, "[Throughout the teshuvah process] we experience many ups and downs. When Hashem feels we've struggled enough, He circumcises our hearts. This is when [the change brought about by teshuvah] becomes permanent."

Food For Thought

When working on personal growth our progress is measured in tiny increments, like a yo-yo, swinging up and down. Sometimes we imagine we're actually getting somewhere. Then, often without warning, we're right back where we started. We might even feel we've regressed. We question why we even bothered. The bliss of ignorance somehow seems more appealing than this emotional roller-coaster that seems to be weaving up and down, getting nowhere fast. However, a time will come — provided we persevere — when we suddenly perceive change. Not just a small change — a massive one. It occurs to us that the *middah* (character trait) that so challenged us is no longer an issue. What only recently seemed so difficult now seems trivial.

Thus, explains the Yismach Moshe, there is the concept of "you will return," meaning the struggle to do so. And when you have struggled and wrestled for long enough, then "Hashem will circumcise your hearts" and you will experience a paradigm-shift. This is all provided, as the verse stipulates, that you first did whatever you could "with all your heart and all your soul."

INSPIRATION

There is a lot of pain associated with working very hard and not seeing progress. Someone trying to quit smoking, for example, often goes through many stages, at times thinking he's conquered his addiction, only to suddenly feel the craving once again. At those times, he feels

> as if all his previous efforts were useless, as if he's gotten nowhere, and his cravings and desires are just as strong. Sometimes this frustration causes him to give up.
>
> But if he sticks to his resolve, and fights his desire over and over again, even though it seems as if he's gotten nowhere, at some point a strange thing will happen. A day, a week, and a month will go by during which he realizes he has not had any serious cravings. Thinking back, it will not be clear to him exactly when or how this happened. One week things were just as difficult as always, and the next it's over, as if he never smoked to begin with.

That's why the Torah refers to the culmination of teshuvah as "finding." You may have exerted much effort in the struggle, but in the end, you suddenly "find" yourself a new person, without ever quite realizing exactly when or how the actual change took place.

As we struggle blindly through a process that is sometimes difficult, we must nevertheless rest assured that one day, without warning, we will receive Heavenly assistance, and all those efforts will have been well worth it.

Inspiration

"And it shall come to pass, when all these things will come upon you, the blessing and the curse ... and you will return to the L-rd your G-d ... " (Devarim 30:1–2). We

know that trials and tribulations — the "curse" — awaken a person's heart to repentance. But how is it possible that a "blessing" can bring one to repentance? This can be likened to a simple person who rebels against the king. Instead of punishing the man, the king gives him an important position. He brings him into his palace and, little by little, promotes him until he is second only to the king himself. With all the good the king has shown him, the rebel agonizes over how he could possibly have rebelled. How could he have defied such a good and merciful king? We see, then, that the blessings and kindness and mercy awaken a deeper level of repentance than even a punishment could bring.

(The Baal Shem Tov)

"Rebbe, I am a sinner. I would like to return, to do teshuvah," declared the chassid.

Rav Yisroel of Ruzhin looked at the man before him. "So why don't you do teshuvah?"

"Rebbe, I do not know how!" the man cried out.

Rav Yisroel retorted. "How did you know to sin?"

The remorseful sinner answered simply. "I acted, and then I realized that I had sinned." "Well," said the Rebbe, "the same applies to teshuvah. Start repenting and the rest will follow of itself!"

(*Mipi Chassidim*)

Nature of Sin

What constitutes sin? On the simple level, sin means violating the halachah by acts of omission or commission. Our duties are spelled out clearly. The law is defined. To ignore the letter or the spirit of the law, let alone to contravene it — that is sin.

On a deeper level, the meaning of sin is indicated in its Hebrew terminology. The general term for transgression is *aveirah*. It is from the root "*avar*," to pass or cross over, to pass beyond. *Aveirah* means a trespass, a transgression, a stepping across the limits and boundaries of propriety to the "other side."

Other words for sin are *chet, aavon, pesha*. The root of *chet* means to miss, to bear a loss to be diminished. The root of *aavon* means to bend, twist, pervert. The root of *pesha* means to rebel.

Technically *chet* refers to inadvertent sins. Inadvertent sins should not be confused with accidental sins where there is absolutely no culpability, i.e., someone pushed you against a light switch on Shabbos, for such an act does not require repentance. If the sin was inadvertent, why does he require repentance? Unintentional sins require atonement because they often occur as a result of a diminished degree of Fear of Hashem. One who is truly fearful of transgressing mitzvos distances himself from the possibility of sinning accidentally. One who has sinned accidentally must atone for this weakening of his G-d consciousness. His teshuvah is defined as regret for having permitted his awareness of Hashem to fade. This commitment to strengthen his connection with Hashem will enable him to merit Hashem's compassion. (*Beis Elokim, Shaar Ha'teshuvah* 1, by Rabbi Moshe MiTrani)

Avon refers to conscious misdeeds and *pesha* to deliberate acts of rebellion. Thus, sin is a move away from Divinity, away from truth. Our sins separate us from Hashem who is truly our life. They separate us from Torah, our lifeline, that which attaches us to the source of our life and all blessings. To neglect the commandments is to deprive ourselves of the illumination and vitality which they provide. When we do so, we forfeit an opportunity, and find ourselves diminished, deficient, and lost.

The Ramban compares sin to a stain. To violate the prohibitions is to defile the body, to blemish the soul, to cause evil to become attached to the person, to detrimentally affect the world at large.

> *One Shabbos, the edge of the Rebbe Reb Boruch of Mezibuzh's* shtreimel *accidentally banged into the ceiling chandelier, sending it swinging. When he saw what had happened he was so distressed that he fainted. After he was revived, he was asked why he*

was so badly affected by an accidental "tiltul min ha'tzad." The Rebbe replied, "It wasn't the sin that troubled me but the contamination which settles on a sinner dimming the soul's spiritual light and distancing the Shechinah.*"*

(Shuva Yisroel, pg. 129–130)

Food For Thought

"Thus do You teach the sinner the way to go" [*Tehillim* 25:8] refers to Hashem showing the way to repentance. Wisdom was asked, "What should be the punishment for the sinner?" She answered, "Let evil pursue the sinner."

(*Mishlei* 13:21)

Prophecy was asked, "What should be the punishment for the sinner?" She answered, "The soul that sins shall perish."

(*Yechezkel* 18:4)

The Torah was asked, "What should be the punishment for the sinner?" She answered, "Let him bring a sacrifice, and be atoned for."

The Holy One, Blessed be He, was asked, "What should be the punishment for the sinner?" He answered, "Let the sinner repent and he will find atonement." This is the meaning of the verse, "Thus You show the sinner the way" — You show the sinner how to repent.

(*Tehillim* 25:8, *Yerushalmi, Makos* II)

Sin offers man temporary gains, but it is altogether shameful, irrational, self-defeating. It is attractive and sweet at the outset, but bitter in the end.

Thus our Sages teach "No person will commit a sin unless a spirit of folly has entered into him" (*Sotah* 2). Sin is an act of ignorance or foolishness. Invariably it can be traced to ignorance, to negligence or carelessness. If premeditated it is outright stupidity. Either way, when an observant Jew sins, his sin is rooted in heedlessness, in shortsightedness, in failure to think. It follows on a blinding obsession with the here and now. A person should weigh the momentary enjoyment against the bitterness of his soul in the World to Come. He will not be able to repent properly if he does not contemplate how disgraceful his deeds are. He must also be conscious of the fact that Hashem will certainly punish him for each evil deed, for nothing is hidden from Hashem and all is recorded before Him. (*Machaneh Yisroel*, pg. 59–60)

Inspiration

The Alter of Kelm points out that the *yetzer hara* is like a dog, but sin is like an angry dog. It is possible to deal with a dog but an angry dog is in an entirely different category and must be dealt with differently. (*Mussar Ve'daas*, pg. 231)

The accusing angel created from the sin vociferously demands sustenance. He is out to annihilate us. (*Tomer Devorah* 1:2) Therefore it behooves us to rid ourselves of this enraged creature as soon as we can.

The Nature of Sin

A habitual sinner is like a person bogged down in a swamp. Slowly but surely his ability to see the truth is lost because of the increasing contamination that clouds his mind, for his sin flits around him providing additional opportunities to transgress.

> *Rav Eliyahu Dushnitzer told the story of a dybbuk that held those present spellbound with his terrifying descriptions of the destructive angels ready to tear him apart if he left the body of the woman in whom he had taken refuge. The next moment he was shouting obscenities, which made those present cringe and cover their ears. When the soul was asked how a dybbuk from the World of Souls could still use such profanities, he explained that if a person doesn't do teshuvah during his lifetime, his soul is not readily weaned of its evil tendencies. How horrifying!*
>
> *(Nachlas Eliyahu)*

The Principle of Teshuvah

If sin was final, the history of mankind would have begun and ended with Adam. Humanity could not survive without teshuvah. Although Hashem desired to create the world based on a system of strict justice, to ensure that it would endure He caused the attribute of Mercy to precede the attribute of Justice and allied them. Hashem would not bring a world into existence if its doom was foreordained (*Ran*).

The body per se is neither evil nor impure, although it is material, and thus attracted to the allure of the physical world. Hashem endowed us with a soul, which is spiritual, and by its very nature it reaches out to, and strives for, spirituality. The actions and behavior of the body-soul fusion, determine whether it will be defiled or ascend to holiness. The Creator takes into account that "sin crouches at the door" (*Bereishis* 4:7), and that "there is no man so righteous on the earth that he does good and never sins" (*Koheles* 7:20). Hashem knows that the inborn inclination of people is to sin and that by nature they gravitate towards the material rather than the spiritual. Therefore He has provided us with teshuvah to ensure the very survival of mankind.

Because Hashem wants to be close to His creatures it was important to provide them with a mechanism that would always enable them to realign their relationship with Him. When the Holy One, blessed be He, created teshuvah, he said to it, as it were, "I am about to create human beings in the world, but on condition that when they turn to you because of their sins, you shall be ready to erase their sins and to atone for them!" The association between teshuvah and the creation of the world signifies that when a person does teshuvah he is starting afresh. The relationship between man and Hashem is recreated.

Inspiration

Hashem's right Hand is extended to receive those who return (*Pesachim* 119). The reason it must be extended is to countermand the attribute of *din* (*Menoras Ha'maor*, Introduction to the Fifth Candle). The right Hand, which signifies Compassion, must overrule the attribute of Judgment, which demands that the person should be punished. (*Nefesh Yehudah*, ibid.)

Mercy means to recognize the legitimacy of justice, yet to show compassion — to forgive nonetheless. Mercy means to recognize the valid demands of the law, but also to temper these demands by considering the fact that "the drive of man's heart is evil yet from his youth" (*Bereishis* 8:21; also see *Bereishis* 5:5).

Mercy means that even a little effort is viewed as monumental. It offers another chance to correct the error of our thoughts, repair the damage, and be spared the consequences of our misdeeds (See *Beis Elokim, Shaar Ha'teshuvah* 1).

> ### Food For Thought
>
> Teshuvah is one of the seven special items created before the world. The others were the Torah, *Gan Eden*, *Gehinnom*, Hashem's Holy Throne of Glory, the *Beis Ha'mikdash*, and the name of *Moshiach*. Rabbi Abahu bar Zeira said, "Great is teshuvah, for it preceded the Creation of the world. As it says, 'Before the mountains were born ... You reduced Man to nothingness, and said "Repent" ... '" (*Tehillim* 90:23).
>
> (*Bereishis Rabbah* 1)

Man is granted the power to make of himself whatever he likes, in effect to determine his immortality. This is possible because man is endowed with free will, while being exposed to temptation. The possibility of many alternatives is what allows for our ultimate self-realization.

The observance of Torah and mitzvos unite the body and the soul, actualizing inherent potentiality, producing a meaningful entity. The *neshamah*, the soul, a spark of G-dliness within us, fills us with practically unlimited potential. This world is the place for growth, for self-improvement, for making changes in our behavior. The World to Come is the place of reward. The nature and quality of the reward are dependent on what one has accomplished in This world. Change and continued growth are no longer possible in the World to Come.

> ### Inspiration
>
> Teshuvah ensures that people will examine their behavior constantly, straighten out their crooked ways, and return to Hashem. "It is impossible for a person not to err or sin, either because he errs in judgment, or because he adopts an undesirable character trait, or because he is overcome by his passions or his anger. If a person believed that he could never rectify his crooked ways he would continue repeating his error, and he might even increase his rebellious acts, as he would have no remedy. However, our faith in teshuvah will cause us to improve, to return to the best of ways and to become more perfect because we sinned." (*Moreh Nevuchim* 3:30) The belief in teshuvah leads to a state that is better, nearer to perfection, than that which he achieved before he sinned.

When Rabbi Yosef Yitzchok Schneersohn, the Lubavitcher Rebbe, reached marriageable age, he was faced with having to choose between several prospective brides. One of those suggested was the young Nechama Dina, daughter of Rabbi Avraham Schneersohn of Kishinev, the son of the Rebbe of Nezhin, who was distantly related to him.

The prospective bridegroom's father, the Rebbe Rashab [Rabbi Shalom Dov Ber, the fifth Chabad Rebbe], was in favor of this match, but the grandmother, Rebbetzin Rivkah, had other plans.

The Rebbe Rashab said to his mother, "Let us follow the advice of the Torah, and ask the boy himself what he wants to do." They called in the young Yosef Yitzchok, gave him the names of all the possible matches, and told him to make the decision for himself.

Yosef Yitzchok replied, "When Avraham sought a wife for his son Yitzchok, he sent his servant Eliezer to his own kinsmen to find a suitable match, saying, 'You shall go to my father's house, and to my kindred, and take a wife for my son.'" Evidently, Yosef Yitzchok had decided to marry his distant relative, Nechama Dina.

Now in those days, it was Rebbetzin Rivkah's custom to distribute honey cake to everyone in the community on the day before Yom Kippur. *Her son, the Rebbe Rashab, would be the first to receive a piece, after which all the chassidim and townspeople would file past her and be given a piece of cake and her blessings for a good and sweet year.*

That year, during which the match between Yosef Yitzchok and Nechama Dina was arranged, the Rebbe Rashab came to his mother as usual for the honey cake before Yom Kippur. *On that occasion, however, he asked for her forgiveness, as the match had not been made according to her wishes.*

Rebbetzin Rivkah responded with the following story:

There was once a Jew living in an isolated settlement, with few Jewish neighbors, who wanted to spend Yom Kippur *in a nearby town in order to daven properly with a minyan. Many such isolated Jewish families would relocate before* Rosh Ha'shanah *and* Yom Kippur *in order to be able to spend the holidays with their brethren. The man informed his wife and family that they would be making the trip into town on the day before* Yom Kippur*, and asked them to ready themselves for the journey.*

When it came time to leave, however, he was the only one ready. The rest of the family had not yet finished packing and making preparations.

He tried to hurry them, as it was Erev Yom Kippur*, but it was obvious they would not be leaving for some time. The man therefore suggested that he start out on the journey himself, walking slowly, so that they would later be able to catch up with him. The entire family would meet at a particular tree and continue on their way together.*

The father set off alone and soon reached the location where they were supposed to meet. Tired by his long walk (and by the drink of schnapps he had downed that morning), he decided to rest in the inviting shade of the tall tree. Lying down on a comfortable spot not visible from the main road, the man soon fell asleep and dozed for many hours.

Meanwhile, the other family members were hurrying along, trying to reach town before sundown. By the time they reached the tree near which their father was fast asleep they had quite forgotten about their agreement, and passed him right by.

Towards evening the man woke up from his nap. Seeing the advancing shadows, he realized that he would never be able to reach the town before dark, nor would he be able to return home without transgressing the holiest day of the year. He would have to spend Yom Kippur *where he was, in the middle of nowhere, under the open sky.*

Lifting his eyes to heaven, the man cried out, "Master of the Universe! My children have totally forgotten about me! I hereby forgive them; now You must forgive Your children who have forgotten about You!"

Rebbetzin Rivkah finished her story with the following words addressed to her son, the Rebbe Rashab: "May Hashem forgive all of us the same way that I have forgiven you."

Definitions of Teshuvah

"What exactly is repentance?" asks the Rambam. *Chovos Ha'levavos* defines teshuvah in terms of self-repair: "Teshuvah is the repair of man's breach in the Divine law after he has strayed from it" (Feldheim translation, pg. 216). It involves dramatic change.

The sinner's mind is shaped by self-gratification and its associated pleasures. His relationship with people and the world around him is calculated to further his agenda of sin. He rallys all the resources of his brainpower and personality in the pursuit of his indulgences. Because so much of his energies are directed towards sinning, when he decides to repent he must recreate himself. Of necessity, he must redirect his mental energies and physical drives, weaving together a whole new tapestry of total devotion to Hashem. (*Le'prakim*, Rabbi Yechiel Yaakov Weinberg)

"Repentance is forsaking sins, removing such thoughts from one's way of thinking, and resolving firmly never to do the sinful thing again" (*Hilchos Teshuvah* 2:2). The act of sin diminishes the sinner, engendering a tolerance for evil and, eventually, distaste for good. According to the Ramban, teshuvah is synonymous with cleansing. Teshuvah purifies the sinner and corrects the flaws that were caused by the sin.

The second dimension of teshuvah is *returning* to Hashem. This is the literal meaning of the word teshuvah. It involves approaching Hashem from the distance of sin as we atone for having angered him (*Beis Elokim, Shaar Ha'teshuvah* 2:1). Teshuvah is "coming home," a reunion. It involves breaching the barrier the sinner has created between himself and Hashem. It is a restoration of a stolen object. When a person does teshuvah he is like a thief restoring the stolen object — in this case, his own soul — to its Source. (Shlah quoting the Ari Ha'kadosh; *Hilchos Teshuvah*)

The Reishis Chochmah equates teshuvah with fear, as in upgrading our fear of Hashem. When a person sins, he casts away his fear. The Ridvaz equates transgression with ignoring our obligation to fear Hashem.

The Kli Yakar suggests that teshuvah lies in doing a mitzvah that is the precise opposite of the transgression, "because through this means he will repair his waywardness" (*Bereishis* 4:16).

People think that teshuvah is only for sinners. But even the perfectly righteous person must do teshuvah — i.e., "return" — to elevate his perfect past to the level of his more perfect present. (Rabbi Shneur Zalman of Liadi)

Definitions of Teshuvah

> ### Food For Thought
> "Teshuvah corrects everything — it rectifies above, rectifies below, rectifies the penitent, and rectifies the whole universe."

The word teshuvah can be read as "*tashuv-hey*" — returning, restoring the *hey* — for when man sins he causes the letter *hey* to be removed from the Divine Name. When this happens, the Divine Name, the manifestation of G-dliness, is no longer whole. The *hey* has been severed, leaving the other three letters to spell *hoy*, the Biblical exclamation for woe.

Note that the letter *hey* represents the physical world: this world was created with the *hey*, because it is like an exedra (closed on three sides and open on the fourth). Whosoever wishes to go astray may choose to let himself fall through the open bottom of the *hey*.

And why is the "leg" of the *hey* suspended leaving an opening at the side, from above? To indicate that whosoever repents is permitted to re-enter.

"Woe to them that call evil good and good evil.... woe to them that they are wise in their own eyes ..." (*Yeshaya* 5:20–21). By contrast, "He who does teshuvah causes the *hey* to be restored ... and the Redemption depends on this" (*Tomer Devorah*, ch. 1, attribute 7).

After a person has sinned, his soul should be overwhelmed by remorse at having distanced himself from Hashem, separating the four letters of Hashem's name and forcing the last *hey* of Hashem's name to sustain the negative forces. Teshuvah restores the *hey*, completes the Holy Name, re-establishes unity, frees the soul. (See *Tomer Devorah*, Attribute 7.)

Teshuvah is the Divinely prescribed remedy for one who has violated a prohibition. All forms of teshuvah, however diverse and complex, have a common core: the belief that human beings have it in their power to effect inward change. Many factors conspire to distance one from the Creator, there remains teshuvah: the ever-present possibility of changing one's life and the very direction of one's life.

> *The repentance of Dr. Nosson Birnbaum, the first prominent secular Jew who became Torah observant, is a good example of this type of teshuvah. The initial revelation came to him, according to his testimony, one wintry night while on an ocean voyage crossing the Atlantic to the United States. He experienced an eye-opener of epic proportions, which the Chazon Ish describes as a clarion call to the refined person free from the hunger of physical distractions who will actually feel impelled by the natural environment to seek out the world's Designer. (See* Emunah U'bitachon.*)*
>
> *Dr. Birnbaum writes: "While all the passengers had sought shelter in their rooms I remained alone on deck looking at the sea, at its rough waves. I raised my eyes heavenward and looked at the myriad of twinkling stars, at the yellowish-silvery glow of the moon, and I listened to the roaring of the water in the ship's wake. Thus, through the wondrous*

sight and moving sound, I suddenly felt a surge of longing for the unknown ... If I could only.... What? I felt that something was missing. The sea beeze was so exhilarating, but my soul was bottled up and could not breathe it. The moonlight shone so brilliantly upon the waves, but my soul was unable to see it. The fur wrap which I had snuggled into no longer warmed me. My soul remained cold to it all. Slowly the sensation of longing turned to fear.

"The ship danced upon the waves, far, far from shore. An ocean of water leaped under it; the sky filled the horizon overhead. The wailing of the wind, the rushing of the waves, and the whisper of the cold-merged into an indescribable tune. 'Oh! Oy Vey! My G-d! What is happening here [What is expected of me?]' I shouted soundlessly. The moon appeared like a face mocking and rebuking me at once. Its confused eyes looked, yet did not look at me. My limbs froze and I almost lost my balance. I cannot recall how long this scene took. I do remember that suddenly everything seemed calm and serene. The moon cast a peaceful light upon me and I felt good, as if nothing had happened. I no longer felt, saw, or heard anything. Silently, I returned to my cabin and only on the morrow was surprised at myself, trying to recapture that singular experience."

For close to ten years, Reb Nosson fought with himself until he freed himself from all doubts and returned to his people. From a sworn atheist he became a fervent believer. He made amends for his *past, not through self-mortification and fasting, but by spreading the Jewish faith and strengthening it in writing and speech.*

(Excerpted from *Those Who Returned*, pg. 255–269)

The Dynamics of Teshuvah

Where does the enormous potency of teshuvah come from? How can it make the sin disappear, recreate the past, as it were? The power of teshuvah derives from its transcendent nature. Because teshuvah preceded the Creation, it is not part of the world of Creation, of a creative process. It is beyond time, beyond space, rooted in infinity. Since teshuvah is not part of a gradual process and development, it is not subject to any order, to the "bureaucracy" of a normative procedure. In the sphere of infinity, past and present fade into oblivion.

It works almost like light. Where does the darkness go when we turn on the light? The *Zohar* tells us that the light absorbs the darkness. Relating this to our sins, our indiscretions are swallowed up by our repentance.

When a person is steeped in wickedness, repentance is like trying to light a candle in an underground dungeon. Lack of oxygen makes this a difficult feat. Thoughts of repentance will often flicker and die out in the heart of a wicked person. He must flee his environment to light the candle of repentance. This usually happens as a result of suffering. (Rav Nochum of Chernobyl)

Concerning a sin committed in error, the Baal Shem Tov explains that when a person repents he places himself on another level of consciousness. Essentially what the person is saying is, "What I know now I was previously unconscious of." One then rises to a higher level, in which his past, deliberate sins are considered to be mere mistakes. That which was previously considered an action performed in full awareness is now revealed as having been performed in ignorance.

A sinner who increases his awareness of Hashem and is inspired to do teshuvah thereby emends his key fault of ignoring Hashem's will because he was not conscious that "there is none besides Him." The very sin he committed is now leading to an increased awareness of Hashem's unity. When connected to Hashem's unity one rises to a higher place where man's sins can be converted to merits. (*Machsheves Mussar*)

Inspiration

"When one returns in teshuvah, he releases all the holiness that he handed over to the forces of evil and restores them to holiness. This is [true] repentance, that one restores a thing to its rightful place. His reward [for doing so] is multiplied greatly because he subdues the forces of evil and releases the holiness from within them. He [thus] gives power to holiness when he brings it inside himself. With this will, we understand what our Sages have

> taught (*Yoma* 86b) that, "one's sins are turned into one's merits."
>
> (*Shaar Ha'yichudim* 3:11, 40b)

When a person is forced by circumstances to commit an act, sometimes it is difficult to ascertain which plays a larger role in his decision to take action: situations beyond his control or his own desires and needs. When he demonstrates that he truly desires that his sins be erased, by not sinning when he is tempted again, it is clear that when he sinned the first time it was mainly because of circumstance and not out of his true free will.

The act of teshuvah reaffirms that his spiritual self never fully participates in the transgression and this reaffirmation in turn causes the sin to become uprooted. (Maharal, *Nesiv Ha'teshuvah*)

Food For Thought

The Rebbe Reb Zusha of Anipoli said that the letters of the word "teshuvah" allude to five paths of repentance.

Taf — stands for *tamim*: "Be sincere with Hashem your G-d." Repentance through sincerity and seriousness, as is said of Avraham, "You found his heart faithful before You."

> *Shin* — stands for *shivisi*: "I have set Hashem before me always." Repentance stemming from man's realization that Hashem creates the whole world every moment ex nihilo.
>
> *Vov* — stand for *ve'ahavta*: "Love your fellow as yourself." Repentance that comes from a good heart.
>
> *Veis* — stands for *Ve'chol*: "In all your ways, know Him." One who considers the events of his life cannot fail to discern the guiding and shaping hand of Divine providence. This awareness inspires repentance.
>
> *Hey* — stands for *hatznei*: "Walk modestly with your G-d." A person must be discreet and hide his piety from observers.

Many factors conspire to distance a person from the Creator, like education and habit. It is difficult to extricate oneself all at once from both the inward and outward consequences of one's actions. One transgression creates a situation in which a second seems logical, natural, and virtually inevitable. A way of life remote from religious observance makes observance difficult. Yet, despite these behavioral tendencies, there remains teshuvah: the ever-present possibility of changing one's life and the very direction of one's life.

> *The Jews of the tiny shtetl near the town of Ushamir suffered terribly under the heavy hand of the dictatorial manager of the lands they leased.*

He worked them to the bone, and nothing they did ever pleased him. Things were bad enough in normal times, but when he decided to vent his rage, life became completely unlivable, for the manager would cut their salaries without a second thought.

This manager was, sad to say, actually a Jew. No one knew where he had come from or what his past was, but it was clear that his tie to Judaism was in his origin only.

It was the week before Rosh Ha'shanah *and the tzaddik Rabbi Mordechai Dov of Hornisteipel arrived in Ushamir for Shabbos. It was his custom during Elul to travel through all the nearby towns and villages to arouse the hearts of the people to the worship of the Creator and urge them to return to Him in full repentance.*

Hundreds of Jews from all the neighboring settlements streamed to Ushamir to spend Shabbos with the great tzaddik. Among them were many Jews from the nearby shtetl. After Shabbos, the people had an opportunity to speak to the tzaddik to receive his blessings.

The residents of the next village decided that this would be a chance to tell Reb Mordechai Dov about the manager. With great sorrow, the tzaddik listened to their heartbreaking story. He was particularly distressed when he heard that the man was a Jew. "Wait till tomorrow, and we'll see what is possible to do," the tzaddik told them.

The next day, right after Shacharis, *Reb Mordechai Dov told his attendant to get the carriage ready for a trip. The tzaddik ordered the driver to turn the horses in the direction of the neighboring village. The inhabitants of the village, who were at that very moment preparing to return home, were very surprised.*

In great haste, they, too, jumped into their wagons and followed the tzaddik. A veritable caravan of wagons set out, the carriage of Reb Mordechai Dov leading the way.

When the caravan reached the neighboring village, the tzaddik inquired where the manager lived and instructed his driver to proceed there. When the villagers saw the caravan with the tzaddik in the lead, they emerged from their homes and stood outside in anticipation. All the while, the tzaddik was very withdrawn, saying nothing.

When they saw from afar the large and beautiful mansion which was the residence of the land manager, all the people drew to a halt. "What is the tzaddik going to do?" they wondered. "What will he say to that wicked one?" they asked one another. "Perhaps with one gaze of his holy eyes, he will turn the manager into a pile of bones," they thought, hopefully.

Standing on the porch, watching the scene, in all his glory, pipe in mouth, stood the land manager, his entire appearance reeking of arrogance.

Yet, as the caravan approached his house, one could see the questioning look of wonder cross his face: What was the meaning of this procession?

Reb Mordechai Dov asked that his carriage halt just in front of the house. Behind him stretched a long line of wagons as far as the eye could see. The tzaddik lifted his eyes and beheld the beautiful mansion. He noticed that the manager was studying him intently. The tzaddik looked in his direction with a steady and unwavering gaze.

Reb Mordechai Dov got down from the carriage and walked toward the mansion. The others, eyes focused on the tzaddik, didn't budge. Reb Mordechai Dov reached the door and after a few seconds, the manager opened the door. The tzaddik and his attendant entered the house. Only a few minutes passed and the tzaddik and his attendant left the house, climbed on the wagon and departed.

What happened inside, the people heard later from the attendant who reported that from the moment the manager had opened the door and until they departed, not one single word was spoken! With a small nod, the manager motioned for them to enter and pointed to a chair for the tzaddik to sit on. He then sat opposite them.

The tzaddik put both hands on the table, straightened his back, and lifted his pure eyes, to look directly into the eyes of the evil dictator. At first, the manager returned his gaze with a hard, defiant look. But gradually as the seconds turned into minutes, his gaze began to soften.

The gaze of the tzaddik, however, which had started off soft and merciful, gradually became deeper and harsher. Then, the eyes of the manager grew moist; a large tear rolled down his cheek. At *that moment the tzaddik rose, and without a word walked to the door. The manager remained motionless in his seat, as if nailed to his place, unable even to accompany his guest to the door. That day the tzaddik remained in the village.*

Everyone who had not been in Ushamir that Shabbos now was able to receive the tzaddik's blessing. Towards evening, when the house in which the tzaddik was staying had emptied of all the people, a bowed figure was seen approaching the house. It was the manager.

He entered the house in an agitated state. For the next two hours he was closeted with the tzaddik. That Rosh Ha'shanah *a new and unexpected worshipper appeared in shul. It was, of course, the manager.*

During the holiday, he stood practically motionless, wrapped in a tallis, praying, and weeping copious tears. From that day on, the estranged and despotic man changed into a true repentant and a friend of his fellow Jews.

(Mipi Chassidim)

The Need to Repent

No matter how many good deeds one has accrued, one is still held accountable for those sins for which he has not repented — and his soul remains tainted by them. Only teshuvah can erase the sins of the past and enable us to begin anew. The teshuvah process is meant to atone for disobeying Hashem and for creating a partition between us and Hashem. Sin disturbs the balance of the universe, destroying its unity. "He who transgresses the precepts of the Torah causes a defect, as it were, above; a defect below; a defect in himself; a defect to all worlds" (*Zohar*).

Teshuvah must be done for all transgressions, whether of a positive or negative mitzvah, whether deliberate or accidental (*Hilchos Teshuvah* of the Rambam). Someone who does teshuvah in words but not in deeds accomplishes nothing. If one doesn't actually work to discard negative behavior, it's hypocritical. Lip service is meaningless.

One also has to do teshuvah for sins not involving any action, such as *lashon hara*, lies, flattery, abusive language, as well for as heretical thoughts. Bad character traits also have to be repented for.

> ### Food For Thought
>
> Rav Yehudah Leib Chasman always wondered why the laws of teshuvah are not widely studied. When a boy becomes a bar mitzvah he prepares for the mitzvah of tefillin by learning the halachos. Each *Yom Tov* we study the halachos that pertain to that *Yom Tov*. These mitzvos are done once a day or once a year. The mitzvah of teshuvah applies at all times, so why aren't we more familiar with the particulars of these laws?
>
> (Ohr Yahel)

We should be conscious of the need for regular repentance. Every time we catch outselves straying, we should immediately return to the straight and narrow path.

> *Rabbi Mendel Futerfas asked a tightrope walker for the secret of his success. He answered, "Keep your destination in focus. Keep your eyes on the other side. But do you know what the hardest part is? "The center?" asked Reb Mendel. "No" replied the tightrope walker. "It is the moment you make the turn and for a fraction of a second you lose sight of your destination."*

Food For Thought

A person who doesn't repent will experience darkness in This World and in the World to Come.

(*Emes Ve'emunah*, pg. 52)

The Gerrer Rebbe once met a young man who told him he was learning at Ohr Somayach in Jerusalem. The young man was quick to add, "But I am not a baal teshuvah." Withough hesitating, the Rebbe asked, "Why not?"

Food For Thought

But He, being full of mercy, forgives sin and does not destroy.

(*Tehillim* 78:38)

Return, you backsliding children, and I will keep you from backsliding.

(*Yirmiyahu* 2:22)

Return to Me and I will return to you.

(*Malachi* 3:7)

Turn to the One against Whom you have rebelled.

(*Yeshaya* 31:6)

Hashem said, "I will forgive as you have asked."

(*Bamidbar* 14:20)

The Teshuvah Process

Many causes motivate a person to do teshuvah: tribulations, rebuke, and old age are some of the factors. A person may return because his current situation does not present him with the opportunity to sin, or because he finds it increasingly embarrassing to let himself be governed by his evil inclination. Little by little he turns away from his sinful ways and returns to Hashem.

A person who was evil his entire life, and does teshuvah at the very end, will discover that none of his misdeeds will be held against him. Teshuvah in old age is a lower level of teshuvah, for one is no longer strong enough to pursue a sinful life. Yet even the teshuvah of the elderly is significant because they have to break out of the restraints of habit. In old age it is hard to change one's ways. (*Avodas Pnim*) The lowest level of teshuvah is that which takes place in the face of impending death.

The different types of teshuvah can be compared to a ship full of people who had spent a long time at sea without reaching their destination.

One day, there was a hurricane at sea. The winds swept the ship and its passengers along, finally depositing them on a small island. The sea surrounded them on all sides, as far as the eye could see.

On the island there were very tall trees heavily laden with fruit, with all kinds of exotic delicacies. Each kind of fruit was beautiful to behold and delicious to eat. The island had sweet springs of water that gushed forth and irrigated the entire island. It was lush with plants and grass. Its flowers bloomed. Its trees sprouted shoots and twigs that grew into branches clothed in a luxuriant growth of leaves. And on these branches were perched many species of beautiful birds that filled the air with their chirping and warbling. It would be delightful to live in such a place in the shade of the tall trees among the springs of sweet water.

There were five groups of people on the ship. The first group refused to get off the ship and onto the island. They said, "If we leave the ship it is possible that another wind will come along and carry off the ship, stranding us on the island. We would be putting ourselves in jeopardy for the momentary pleasure of enjoying the fruits of the island. If the ship goes off and we are left on the island, we will die."

The second group disembarked from the ship onto the island, but they did not spend much time there. They tasted some of the fruit, strolled briefly about the island, and immediately returned to the ship. They found the same seats that they had left and settled comfortably into them. They suffered no loss for having visited the island.

The third group also disembarked from the ship. They ate from the fruits of the trees, and they strolled about the island. They stayed on the island until a stiff wind arose. The crew of the ship wanted to set sail and continue their voyage. The sailors sounded the customary departure signals on their bugles. When this group heard the sound of the bugles they immediately became concerned for their safety and hurried back to the ship. They still managed to find places to sit but not with the same comfort as the first and second group.

The fourth group ate from the fruits of the trees and swam in the waters of the island. When they heard the sounds of the bugles they said, "Although they have sounded the bugles, they will not leave until they erect the mast. Once the mast was erected they said, "They still won't go until they have unfurled the sails."

Once the sails were unfurled they said, "Surely they won't go until the sailors have eaten."

All the while these people were sitting and eating the fruit of the island, intoxicated with the wine of their desires. Meanwhile, the sailors finished eating, manned their positions, and the ship set sail.

Once the ship set sail, however, this group said, "If we delay one moment longer the ship will leave without us, and we will be doomed."

They immediately ran to the shore and leaped recklessly into the sea. They swam to the ship and climbed into it. The places they found for themselves were cramped and uncomfortable, unlike those of the people who had not dallied so long on the island.

The fifth group made themselves comfortable on the island. They ate, drank, and made merry. They gave absolutely no thought to returning to the ship until it was already gone and they were left marooned on the island. The summertime passed, and the winter arrived in its stead. The fruits fell off the trees. The leaves withered on the branches. The people were left unprotected from the blistering sun during the day and from the freezing cold in the night. Strange and vicious beasts emerged from their lairs and attacked them. They cried and lamented that they had not returned to the ship, but it was to no avail. They remained on the island and perished. In the final analysis, they were cut off both from the ship and the island.

This is analogous to the situation in which a person finds himself in This World. His good deeds are like the ship in which he travels through his life. If he conducts himself with integrity and serves his Creator meticulously, not allowing his evil inclination to tempt him into the empty pursuits of the world, he is assured of reaching his destination safely.

The first group, who refused to get off the ship altogether, represents the thoroughly righteous people who have never tasted sin, who have overcome their evil inclination and spurned the material lure of this world. These people never left their places to set foot on the island; they have never allowed themselves to be influenced by the seductive pull of worldly desires which can ultimately destroy those who indulge.

The second group, who visited the island only briefly, represents those people who sin but do teshuvah immediately, right after they sinned, while they are still in their full youthful vigor, which is the ideal teshuvah.

The third group, who did not leave the island until they heard the sounds of the bugles signaling the impending departure of the ship, represents those people who do teshuvah only when they grow old. When old age arrives, people see their strength waning and consider that their days are numbered. Only when they realize that their time in This World will soon be coming to an end do they give thought to doing teshuvah. Although their teshuvah is also accepted, their places are not as comfortable as those of the first two groups.

The fourth group, who waited until the last second, only leaving the island when the ship had already set sail, represents those people who do teshuvah only on their deathbed. Only when they see death staring them in their faces do they do teshuvah. Although this teshuvah is also acceptable, their station is considerably less comfortable than that of the other groups.

The fifth and final group, who stayed behind on the island and then shed futile tears at their folly, represents the incorrigible sinners. These people are so steeped in their physical desires that they arrogantly reject the very thought of doing teshuvah. They die sinful and are doomed to destruction. The pleasures of This World are replace by the worms and maggots of the grave; their flesh is devoured, their souls consumed. They are condemned to everlasting shame and disgrace. They are as the island dwellers whose idyllic existence is replaced by the most dreadful conditions, who must suffer blistering heat during the daytime and bitter cold at night, who are beset by strange, vicious beasts and by snakes and scorpions. (*Menoras Ha'maor*, Candle 5, section 1, ch. 2–3))

If a person does not repent during his lifetime, teshuvah is no longer possible for him after death.

> *In his youth Reb Shimon ben Lakish was the leader of a robber band. He returned to Hashem wholeheartedly and for the rest of his days he was engaged in the study of Torah and the practice of mitzvos, and his teshuvah was accepted.*
>
> *On the day of his death, two of his erstwhile friends, who had remained robbers, also died. Rebbe Shimon ben Lakish was granted entry into* Gan Eden, *while his two robber friends were consigned to the abyss. They said, "Lord of the Universe! Is there arbitrary preference before You?"*
>
> *Hashem replied, "He repented while still alive and you did not." Said they, "Leave us and we will repent." Said Hashem, "Teshuvah is possible only till the day of death."*

To what is the matter compared? To a person who departs on a sea voyage. If he fails to take along bread and water from the land, he will not find them at sea. Or, to a person headed for a trip through the wilderness. Should he fail to take along bread and water from civilization, he will not find food and drink in the wilderness. Likewise, if a person fails to do teshuvah during his lifetime, teshuvah is no longer possible for him after death. (*Pirkei De'rebbe Eliezer* 43)

> One day during the month of Elul, Reb Levi Yitzchok of Berditchev was making his way home from shul. On his way, he encountered someone known for his many transgressions and aimless lifestyle. Reb Levi Yitzchok stopped him and said: "I am envious of you. These are days of repentance. If you repent wholeheartedly, all your transgressions will be transformed into merits!"

When to Repent

The *Mishnah* in *Pirkei Avos* (2:15) says a person should do teshuvah the day before he dies. But nobody knows when that will be. Therefore, it is appropriate for us to do teshuvah every day. This way a person will always be engaged in holy activities which will lengthen his life. As it says, "Teshuvah lengthens the days and years of a person's life" (*Yoma* 86:2).

Food For Thought

The Jewish year begins and ends with repentance. We conclude the year with the days of *Selichos*, and we begin it with the Ten Days of Repentance.

(Rav Menachem Mendel of Lubavitch)

A person should repent every day before going to sleep, every *Erev Shabbos*, during the Ten Days of Repentance, or, at the very latest, on *Yom Kippur*. Repentance on *Erev Shabbos* readies our soul for Shabbos. (*Ohel Shimon*, pg. 107) *Motzaei Shabbos* is a good time to repent, for one can still attatch oneself to the holiness of Shabbos (Reb Yissochar Dov of Belz, *Admorei Belz*).

Even though repentance and pleading for forgiveness are always appropriate, they are even more fitting in the ten days between *Rosh Ha'shanah* and *Yom Kippur*, when they are accepted immediately. As it is written, "Seek out the Lord while He may be found" (*Hilchos Teshuvah* of the Rambam). The month of Elul is also an auspicious time for doing teshuvah as it is a month which is wholly compassion. (Gra, *Likutim* to *Sefer Ha'yetzirah*)

Inspiration

The Ramchal explains that the connection between Hashem and a person's soul is like the connection between metal and a magnet (*Mesilas Yesharim* 1, end). The metal is always drawn to the magnet. However when they are far apart there is no attraction. The only remedy is to have the magnet draw near the metal so that the attraction is set in motion. This is what Hashem does during Elul. He "lowers Himself," as it were, so that the attraction can resume full force.

(*Le'hair Le'horos u'le'Haskil*, pg. 298)

When to Repent

Every holiday involves preparation. The mitzvah most closely associated with the days leading up to the holiday of *Yom Kippur* is teshuvah. During the Ten Days of Repentance beginning with *Rosh Ha'shanah*, Hashem is on twenty-four-hour call. This is a time for sincere introspection and a careful and honest examination of the record of the outgoing year, with a view to acquiring proper resolutions which are to regulate one's personal daily life, as well as that of his home, and all his affairs in the year to come. How foolish are those who go about their affairs, unaware of their judgment, and occupy themselves with matters other than repentance, finally appearing before Hashem with their shopping list of requests.

> *Reb Tzvi of Portziva used to lead the* Musaf *prayer on* Rosh Ha'shanah *in the synagogue of Reb Yosele of Torchin, the Chozeh of Lublin's son.*
>
> *He was once asked by Reb Yitzchok Meir of Ger: "Perhaps you could repeat for me a teaching which you heard from Reb Yosele?"*
>
> *"At the moment I do not recall any words of Torah," said Reb Tzvi. "But I do remember a story ..."*
>
> *One* Rosh Ha'shanah, *just before the blowing of the shofar, Reb Yosele entered the shul and told his chassidim, some of whom were undoubtedly thinking at that moment of their own requests to the Almighty for the coming year, "I am not going to rebuke you, nor am I going to teach you Torah. I am only going to tell you a story.*
>
> *"In a certain city, a learned and wealthy wine merchant lived, who was honored one day by a visit*

from the local rabbi. The host went out of his way to show the rabbi great respect. The merchant quickly sent his servant down to the cellar, where he was to fill a bottle of wine from the middle barrel of the third row — for this was the best wine he owned. All the while, he engaged in a scholarly conversation with his distinguished guest.

"When the merchant had waited quite a while for his servant to return, he excused himself and quickly descended to the cellar to find out what had happened. He was shocked at what he saw there. Some of the barrels were uncovered; others were being drained, as their taps had been left open; broken bottle were lying in the puddles of wine on the floor; and the servant was nowhere to be seen.

"The merchant returned upstairs, very upset at the serious damage his servant had caused him. He began to look for the servant, calling him by name. The servant finally answered, from a comfortable place over the fireplace, where he was sprawled at his leisure. From up there, the servant called out to his master, 'Listen here! I want you to increase my salary by so and so much. It isn't nearly high enough....'"

Reb Yitzchok Meir of Gur thanked Reb Tzvi warmly. "Now that is what I call a fine parable!" he exclaimed.

Adopting additional stringencies during these days is recommended because we are asking that Hashem relate to us beyond the letter of the law (see *Kitzur Shulchan Aruch* 130).

One must set aside time to be alone to seek out and examine his ways, and occupy himself with repentance. (*Orchos Tzaddikim, Teshuvah*)

The Ramak agrees that at this time one should limit one's usual activities, setting aside special hours during the day and night for introspection and self-examination. The *Chayei Adam* suggests that the best time to focus on the ways of teshuvah, pouring forth our prayers and uttering confessions for our sins, is early in the morning (*Chayei Adam, Teshuvah*).

> *Many of the Sanzer Rav's responsa written after the Days of Awe include a note attributing their delay to his involvement with matters pertaining to the Days of Awe.* (Teshuvos Divrei Chaim) *The Sanzer Rav usually davened in his private* beis medrash. *However, from* Rosh Chodesh Elul *until* Rosh Ha'shanah *he would daven in the city's main shul. The city's Jews were engulfed in awe when they saw the Rav striding towards the main shul on his way to prayers, as they knew that the month of Elul was upon them.*
>
> (*Darkei Chaim*)

There are very few things that are as beneficial to a Jew as the period of teshuvah and Divine forgiveness of the *Yamim Noraim*. On these days we are judged for the past year and Hashem decides how we will be rewarded or, G-d forbid, punished. For this reason the month preceding *Rosh Ha'shanah* — Elul — is a special time for teshuvah. As we approach *Rosh Ha'shanah* it is easy to become dejected when we recall our goals of the past and our limited success in meeting them over the year. But we must remember who we are: "You are children to G-d, your L-rd" (*Devarim* 14:1).

When a rebellious subject desires to come back to the kingdom, the king may opt to punish the transgressor before restoring his citizenship. But a wayward child who returns is welcomed by his parents with open, loving arms. Our Father awaits us. It is *we* who must so choose. Failure to reach out to Hashem at this time of year is not merely negligent, it is insulting. (Rav Itzele Peterburger) As a general rule, our punishment is compounded if we fail to return (see *Shaarei Teshuvah*), but this is especially true prior to *Yom Kippur* when purification comes so easily. It is for this reason that the Rambam emphasizes that the person who is neither totally guilty nor totally innocent should embrace teshuvah. This is the mitzvah which will ensure that we are inscribed for life. (See *Kochvei Ohr*)

Food For Thought

It is very important to remember that everything we do for *Rosh Ha'shanah* and *Yom Kippur*, such as praying, blowing the shofar, fasting, and all of the other mitzvos and customs of this time, will earn us forgiveness for our sins only if they are accompanied by teshuvah. Empty acts will not accomplish this goal.

(Rav Yisroel Salanter)

When to Repent

A student once followed the Chofetz Chaim up to a shul's attic where he went to meditate in solitude in preparation for the upcoming Days of Awe. The student stood on the other side of the closed door and listened to the Chofetz Chaim depict his judgment by the Heavenly Court. He graphically described his merits coming to the fore and testifying on his behalf: from the Torah he learned, from the mitzvos he kept, and from his writings.

He then went on to verbally portray his sins coming forward in large numbers. Counted among his sins were mitzvos performed without the proper intent and mitzvos that he had not embraced with alacrity. He articulated the Shechinah's *response: "Is he alive or dead?" The Chofetz Chaim then concluded, "Let him do teshuvah for his sins as long as he is still alive," and then the Chofetz Chaim started to cry.*

(Derachav, Nimukav Ve'sichosav shel Ha'Chofetz Chaim)

Food For Thought

Rav Yisroel Salanter said, "Most people start doing teshuvah the week before *Rosh Ha'shanah* while some begin the month before. But the best time to start doing teshuvah is immediately after *Yom Kippur*." (In other words, year round.)

The following parable is a dramatization of the dreadfulness of a once-a-year, *Yom-Kippur*-only commitment.

There was once a girl who came of age and met a poor boy she liked. He had no profession, no prospects, and no savings. The girl was not put off. She bought an apartment and furnished it. She opened a joint bank account. She used her money to outfit him for their wedding which of course she paid for. The wedding was magnificent. He looked absolutely breathtaking as he stood under the chuppah.

The morning after the wedding, he went down to the grocery to buy breakfast and never came back.

An hour or two passed and there was no sign of him. She called the grocery only to discover that he had never been there. When it started getting dark she began to worry that something had happened to him. She called the police. They found no evidence of violence. Weeks passed, she could not keep his disappearance a secret. The shame and humiliation she endured seared her soul. The months passed with no letter, no phone calls. The only sign of life were withdrawals from their mutual bank account.

A year of loneliness passed. Many emotions coursed through her. Humiliation followed anger, fear was mixed with pain. The night of her first anniversary, the miserable young woman took out her wedding album and flipped through the pages as the tears soaked the photographs. Suddenly there was a knock at the door. Her husband stood framed in the doorway wearing his wedding outfit. He looked so handsome. Smiling from ear to ear he handed her a bouquet of flowers as he murmured a thousand apologies.

She was dumbfounded. Torn between anger and hopefulness which was fueled by affection, she didn't know whether to show him the door or allow him to start a new page. Should she demand an explanation or simply forget and forgive. He appeared not to notice her silence. "You look pale," he said. "Let's sit down on the couch." And finally, "Why are you so quiet?"

What would you do? How would you react? She decided to swallow her recriminations and ask no questions. She graciously accepted his apology. The next morning he went out to buy some groceries — and did not return.

This time she did not call the police. She did not even tell her parents about the visit. On the eve of the second anniversary she did not take down the wedding album. However, she was not surprised when the bell rang and her former groom stood framed in the doorway dressed in his wedding finery. He had a bouquet of flowers in his hand, a smile on his face, and apologies on his lips.

What would you do? Would you allow him to enter or slam the door in his face?

Let us take one last listen-in on the conversation between the woman and her errant husband. "What do you want," she asks in a voice dripping with acid.

> "I brought you flowers," he replies. "I wanted to ask if you could deposit some money in the bank. There is nothing left and I have a lot of expenses. I am sure you understand...."
>
> (*Maayan Ha'moed, Yom Kippur*)

To be sure, *Yom Kippur* is not a once-a-year obligation to be forgotten after the day is passed. Teshuvah is a year-round obligation. How dare we present ourselves before Hashem with our shopping list of requests without the prerequisite repentance?

Teshuvah draws a person close and suspends judgment but does not purify his soul from the contamination caused by sin, until *Yom Kippur*. In His great mercy, after the sin of the Golden Calf was forgiven, Hashem established this day for forgiveness. (*Yoma* 86a; *Chinuch*, Mitzvah 185) Had He not done so, people's sins would continue to accumulate year after year, eventually reaching a point where they would be too numerous to bear, and the people would then be deserving of annihilation. Repentance enables us to erase the backlog of sin, to make a fresh start. We should feel tremendous gratitude toward the Almighty for the gift of *Yom Kippur*.

Food For Thought

How great is Hashem's compassion! If *Yom Kippur* came only once in seventy years it would be an enormous kindness. We should be overjoyed that we can achieve atonement on a yearly basis.

The numerical equivalent of "*ha'satan*" is 364, one less than 365. This signifies that there is only one day of the year when the *yetzer hara* is powerless — *Yom Kippur*.

(*Arvei Nachal, Emor, Derush* 4)

Suffering and Teshuvah

Some people are inspired to return to Hashem when they hear of the suffering of a friend, as in the case of a servant who has fled from his master, and who returns to him on hearing of the punishment meted out to another who fled. (*Orchos Tzaddikim, Teshuvah*)

When Hashem visits suffering on a person, He is, as it were, imploring him to improve. Indeed, Hashem will periodically remind us of our mortality so that we are prompted to do teshuvah. (*Kav Ha'yashar* 77) When a person receives this type of clear warning from Heaven, he should take it to heart, acknowledge that these troubles are the fruits of his ways and actions, and repent. Yosef's brothers immediately made the connection between being threatened without apparent justification and the deed of selling their brother. They declared, "Hashem has found out the sin of your servants!" (*Bereishis* 44:16)

The person who returns because of suffering is like the servant who has fled and returns after being seized by the secret police who torture him for his insubordination. Even this type of teshuvah is not rejected by Hashem. (*Orchos Tzaddikim, Teshuvah*)

> ### Food For Thought
>
> To say, "This is just how the world runs, and this trouble happened to happen," is an act of cruelty, for it causes a person to persist in his negative ways.... [Rather,] it should serve to rouse the heart and open pathways of return to G-d.
>
> (Rambam)

A ferocious dog broke the chain shackling him and viciously attacked Rav Dovid Bodnick. The dog's owner, who witnessed the assault, could not restrain his dog. For a moment, Rav Dovid sought a branch or stone he could use to stop the dog's biting. He then reminded himself that the dog was simply Hashem's agent, sent to remind him to repent ... at that moment the dog turned away and returned to his master.
(Ha'meoros Ha'gedolim #9)

When an afflicted person does not repent his punishment is increased. If he considers what befalls him as chance happenings, then he will be the object of great wrath. Unfortunate is the person who does not repent, for he has suffered affliction for no purpose and his punishment is doubled because he does not believe that his sins are the cause of his afflictions. (*Orchos Tzaddikim, Teshuvah*)

"When a person accepts upon himself Hashem's reproof and corrects his ways and thoughts, it is fitting that he rejoice over his suffering, for through it he has attained exalted levels of spirituality." (*Arvei Nachal, Be'chukosai, Derush* 5) It is therefore proper for him to offer praise unto Hashem, Blessed is He, as he would for his other successes. Thus it is written, "I will raise the cup of salvation and invoke the Name of Hashem" (*Tehillim* 116:13) and "Trouble and sorrow I would find then I would invoke the name of Hashem" (ibid. 3–4). Punishment is a means to indicate to the person that he has erred and must return. When he acknowledges his deviation from the straight and narrow path then he no longer requires chastisement. (See *Sichos Mussar* 5732, *Miketz*)

INSPIRATION

One sigh from the depths of the heart is dearer to Hashem than all the fasts and suffering of distiniguished scholars.

(Ari Ha'kadosh)

> ### INSPIRATION
>
> The *Tanya* explains: "One definitely repents in the end, in this incarnation or the next, for no one is entirely pushed away." The *mashpia* Rabbi Shmuel Betzalel, when teaching *Tanya* to students of the Tomchei Temimim Yeshivah, would reach this section and break out crying. "*Kinderlach!*" he would say. "You must repent. Ultimately you will be forced to, so what are you waiting for?"
> (*Days of Awe, Days of Joy*, pg. 145)

It is worth noting that sometimes the *baal teshuvah* is challenged with difficult tests to encourage continued growth. The *yetzer hara* is anguished at his exalted spiritual heights and suggests that he is unworthy of such favor. At that point he is forced to prove himself. When he is stretched to the limit by such a test, he should not despair, but remind himself that his persistence will atone for his sins.

These discouraging experiences are necessary to test the *baal teshuvah*'s sincerity. When he is confronted with these trials and stands his ground, continuing to serve Hashem unabashedly, it is an indication that he has properly returned. This steadfast loyalty is very precious to Hashem.

10
Cheshbon Ha'nefesh

If a man aspires to improve his character, and grow spiritually, he must carefully weigh his actions from time to time, subjecting them to searing scrutiny. How has he spent his time? What can he do to spend his time more fruitfully? He must determine the motivations for his every deed. Once he has clarified the motivating factors, he can establish if they are in accordance with the Torah, with the will of Hashem. He must get to know himself well and in accordance with his findings, plan his subsequent life.

Food For Thought

One should never underestimate the power of a genuine sigh. When a person sighs as he is making his spiritual reckoning, this sigh rectifies the deeds which caused his anguish.

(*Ohr Yechezkel, Emunah*, pg. 40; *Mei Ha'shiluach*)

Cheshbon Ha'nefesh

Every night before you go to sleep you should make a reckoning of all the actions you executed during the day and then repent and crave Hashem's indulgence for your shortcomings (*Shaarei Kedushah* 1:6). People who do this are called "men of reckoning" (*Zohar, Bamidbar* 178). This repentance should resume after midnight when one rises to say *Tikkun Chatzos*. If you are not comfortable in the Holy Tongue, you should speak to Hashem in your own language so that you can express your distress without difficulty. (*Ateres Tzvi, Bnei Yissoschar*) This daily reckoning rectifies the deeds of the day so that we do not lose a vital spark that animates our soul (*Taharas Kodesh*).

> Rav Chaim of Admur collapsed one evening before he was about to go to sleep. His followers revived him with difficulty. When they asked him what had happened, he answered: A king had numerous servants, each one of whom was given a different assignment. The king commanded that every night they should all present themselves to him together with all the things they had repaired during the day, and on approval, deposit them in his treasury. The next day he would give them more objects to repair.
>
> Among them was one lazybones who couldn't get himself to begin his task and, in addition, soiled the work clothes he had been given. In the evening, when he saw all his colleagues in their spotless clothes, presenting beautifully repaired items to the king, and he, who was dressed in filthy rags, had nothing

> *to show for himself and nothing to deposit in the treasury, he was taken aback and dumbfounded with shame and disgrace.*
>
> *(Judaism: Thought and Legends, pg. 14, Rabbi Meir Meisels)*

Look back on your thoughts and actions and see whether they constituted a step forward or backward, whether your character showed greater refinement or your thoughts had taken a humbler turn. Without any self-deception and partiality, judge yourself. Do not cover up, but renew your resolution for the morrow to go forward and not backward. (Rav Samson Raphael Hirsch) The Ramchal cries out with great passion that this frequent self-evaluation is the only thing that saves man from *Gehinnom*.

> *Rav Elya Lopian spent a night in a hotel in Rasien. Before Rav Elya fell asleep he could hear a voice he did not recognize reviewing and evaluating the deeds of the day. He was asking himself whether this deed should have been done or avoided or whether it ought to have been done another way.*
>
> *In the morning Rav Elya asked who was sleeping in the next room. When he was told it was Rav Boruch Ber of Kamenitz, he said to himself, "I am considered a* baal mussar *and I went to sleep tranquilly. Reb Boruch Ber is supposedly against the study of* mussar *but engages in an intense spiritual reckoning before putting his head on the pillow.*
>
> *(Ha'rav Domeh Le'malach)*

> *When Reb Moshe Feinstein had to have a pacemaker inserted, he sought to clarify the sin which caused this affliction. He knew that his suffering must be a punishment for hurting someone but he couldn't recall who he might have hurt. He carefully reviewed his lifetime, going back to his childhood. It was there that he found the reason he was now suffering. When he was a child in cheder, he and a friend both supplied the teacher with an answer to his question. Reb Moshe remembered how he felt so proud that his answer was better than his friend's. True he was not responsible for the hurt incurred but his reaction was unbecoming. He had inadvertently brought shame to his friend.*
> (*Reb Moshe* [ArtScroll], by Rabbi Shimon Finkelman and Rabbi Nosson Scherman)

One goal of scrutinizing our actions is to prevent evil habit or shortcomings from taking root. Just as the captains of industry continually reassess management strategies and review the balance sheets to avoid losses, so must we establish regular times for spiritual accounting, until this becomes a permanent feature of our lives. (*Mesilas Yesharim*) Any businessman who does not take inventory will soon find that he will be forced to close shop (*Birchas Avrohom*, pg. 128).

It is never too early, but it is also never too late. This self scrutiny should be conducted in an atmosphere of urgency, as if any moment he may be called to give account of himself before the Arbiter of all.

Rabbi Naftali Nosson Nota Hirsch, dressed in Shabbos clothing, was singing joyously when his soul left this world. He was in the midst of expounding on the verse "Nachpesa darkeinu ve'nachkora — let us search our ways and investigate them" (Eichah 3:40) explaining that the walls of a person's house testify on their behalf. We must search our ways in repentance, and then (nach korah) noach — *it will be pleasant —* koreh *because our beams will testify on our behalf.*

(*Imrei Tzaddikim* 22)

Inspiration

"There is not a person who does not have an hour" (*Pirkei Avos*). Although this verse has been explained in many ways, the Rebbe Reb Elimelech of Lizhensk says the following: A person who does not set aside an hour to meditate on his purpose in this world is not considered a human being (*Noam Elimelech, Parshas Bo*). There is no repentance without meditation. The author of *the Chareidim*, Rabbi Elazar Azkari, quotes the Arizal as advising that one day a week the Torah scholar should go off alone and meditate on standing before Hashem in judgment, and he should speak to Hashem like a servant to his master and a son to his father (*Ohr Le'shav*, pg. 49).

Living with the realization that a person will have to give an accounting of his deeds enables a person to follow the admonition of the Rosh in *Orchos Chaim* (109): "Do not do privately that which you would be ashamed to do publicly, and do not say, 'Who sees me?'"

A person should always live in a way that will make it easier for him to explain his actions to the Heavenly Court after his stay on this earth.

> The completion of the Kamenitz Yeshivah building in Chanukah of 1937 was celebrated with great fanfare. Kamenitz Zionists who had formed an orchestra offered to provide the entertainment at the ceremony at no charge to the yeshivah. The Rosh Yeshivah, Reb Boruch Ber, refused to permit them to participate, telling his confidants that he didn't want his boys looking at their faces. He resisted the musicians' attempts to persuade him otherwise. In order to avoid humiliating the volunteers, they were whisked off to the old building, where they performed for the benefit of those milling around there.
>
> Reb Boruch Ber later explained: "The Rebbe [Rav Chaim of Brisk] said that a Jew must be conscious of eventually giving an accounting of all his deeds. After 120, I will state that I did not permit them to perform for my charges."
>
> (Ha'rav Domeh Le'malach, pg. 390–391)

> **INSPIRATION**
>
> Even the performance of good deeds requires a great deal of introspection. Rabbeinu Bachya writes that he was hesitant at first to take on the task of writing his guide to the development of proper *middos* because he felt that he might have been wrongly motivated by pride. But after honest soul-searching, he saw that laziness might be responsible for this "holy" rationalization and preventing him from writing this classic *mussar* text.
>
> Rabbeinu Bachya, a giant among giants, who wrote the master work on "obligations of the heart," knew how important it is to probe deeply into our subconscious to determine the true motivations behind our thoughts. By delving into and ascertaining our true intentions, we can purify them and thereby improve our actions and make them more meaningful.
>
> (Introduction to *Chovos Ha'levavos*)

While Rav Elya Lopian was in the midst of eye surgery, his blood pressure rose alarmingly high. Although he was near death, with the help of Hashem he slowly recovered, aided by the numerous prayers of many throughout the yeshivah world. The surgeon was never able to explain why Reb Elya's blood pressure suddenly escalated terrifyingly.

Years later he had to have surgery again. The doctor took extra precautions to avoid a recurrence of the previous episode. The second time around there was no incident. During the recovery period, Rav Elya recalled the close call with death in his previous surgery. He explained that he had prepared for surgery with a spiritual reckoning. When they began the procedure, he was still focused on reviewing his deeds, and that was the reason his blood pressure rose. "This time around I was careful to let my mind go blank and that is why my blood pressure remained normal," he explained.

(Introduction to *Lev Eliyahu*)

Food For Thought

Know your soul and you will know your Creator.
(*Toldos Yitzchok, Bereishis*)

Just as the body requires food daily, so the soul continually requires perfecting.
(Abarbanel)

He who knows himself can be expected to know others; he who doesn't know himself will certainly not know others.
(*Olam Katan*)

A yeshivah student who doesn't know what he lacks is blemished. But someone who doesn't know his strong points can't even begin to attempt to serve Hashem.
(Rav Yeruchem Levovitz)

Recognize how many evil character traits you harbor and then acquire the courage, the will, and intense desire to rescue yourself, with Hashem's help, from these enemies of your soul. The knowledgeable person confronts what he lacks, takes advantage of what he has, and spares no effort to move forward.

Shlomo Ha'melech said, "The fool walks in darkness" (*Koheles* 2:14). He sees the darkness of his situation but keeps walking in the dark, with no aspirations to reach the light. Change and improvement don't seem to be a possibility. However wrong he knows he is, he does nothing to change and that will bring about his total destruction. Don't engage in a spiritual reckoning if your mind is unclear (*Erech Apayim*, pg. 68). When engaged in spiritual reckoning, it is important to be on the lookout for the *yetzer hara,* who constantly hovers around us seeking an avenue for destruction. This lesson is brought home by the Ziditchover Rebbe, based on the verse, "And Yosef came into the house to do his work" (*Bereishis* 39:11). The *Targum* translates this as: "He came in to go over the accounts." The Ziditchover explains that Yosef began to make a self-accounting. This cast him into depression, and almost caused him to sin with Potiphar's wife. (*Sur Me'ra* 27b) A person has to be careful not to get depressed over the past or worried about the future. He should simply "snatch" as much Torah and prayer as he can.

When one's introspection effects a real change in attitude, the process of teshuvah has begun.

> *A chassid once bemoaned his wily and scheming character and asked the Lubavitcher Rebbe, the*

Rashab, how to rectify his inclination to do everything with cunning.

The Rebbe advised him to spend fifteen minutes daily on a spiritual reckoning, contemplating his entity and his existence. In addition he recommended that he restrict his speech.

When he related the story to his son, Rav Yosef Yitzchok, the Rebbe Rashab told him that the chassid had become a changed man. He then added, "Don't think I mean that he was a changed man only in regard to his spiritual faculties. I mean a complete transformation, a metamorphosis. If you would have seen him yourself you would have been greatly impressed by the unbelievable difference this commitment made on him. His very nature changed!"

(Rav Yosef Yitzchok of Lubavitch)

Prompt Repentance

The highest level of teshuvah is that which is done right after the offense. Ideally a person should immediately say, "I have sinned before you and angered You. I beseech You, Hashem, have compassion on my unfortunate soul so that my connection with you is not severed!" (*Taharas Ha'kodesh*) Hashem ensures that a person who is quick to repent achieves atonement in this world (ibid.). If one defers repentance, the sins "age" and lose their sting, and one does not worry over them as in the beginning. (*Orchos Tzaddikim, Shaar Teshuvah*)

We must always be prepared to stand before the Heavenly Court for no one knows when his day will come. A wicked person who had died, wanted to be allowed to do teshuvah. He was informed that the World to Come is like Shabbos. Just as a person who does not prepare on *Erev Shabbos* has nothing to eat on Shabbos, so a person who does not rectify his deeds in This World will suffer from deprivation in the World to Come. (*Midrash Rabbah, Koheles* 1:15)

Inspiration

"If it is bent, it cannot be made straight, and if something is missing, it cannot be replaced."

(*Koheles* 1:15)

"In This World, what is crooked can be made straight, and if something is missing, it can be replaced; however, in the World to Come, the opportunity to straighten out the crooked or to replace something that is missing has passed."

(*Koheles Rabbasi* 1)

If one's behavior is "crooked" in some way, it has to be straightened out in This World. Similarly, if one's behavior is lacking an important characteristic, perhaps to develop and exercise greater generosity, the time to work on acquiring and exercising that characteristic is in This World; afterwards, it will be too late.

Reb Yochanan Ben Sakami compares it to a king who invited his servants to a feast without specifying a time. The wise servants got ready and waited at the outside of the palace. Those with less intelligence went about their affairs without giving a thought to the upcoming state dinner. Suddenly the king's servants came to summon them all to the palace. Those waiting at the door were immediately escorted to the king's banquet hall. The others were brought into the king's presence grubby and unprepared. The king welcomed those who were ready for the occasion to sit at his side. The others were forced to stand and watch. (*Shabbos* 153:71)

> ### Inspiration
>
> "Before a decree is issued, a person's prayers and repentance can remove any blemish resulting from his sin. After the decree it is too late."
>
> (*Shaarei Teshuvah*)

Rav Yosef Yoizel, later known as the Alter of Novardok was a successful entrepreneur. One day he met Rav Yisroel Salanter and the two began talking. Reb Yosef Yoizel explained that he had gone to work to support his family because, as he put it, "A person needs to provide the basics for living." Rav Yisroel Salanter looked at him and replied, "You're busy looking for something to live with but what have you prepared to die with?"

Rav Yosef Yoizel was deeply affected by these words. He went straight home, sold his business, settled all his affairs, shut himself in a little hut in the forest, and studied full time for fourteen years.

Moshiach will arrive and then it will be too late, for in the Messianic era, repentance will not be accepted (*Rashba, Shabbos* 151b; *Maharil* 153a). Knowing that *Moshiach* is coming, we should force ourselves to repent immediately.

This can be compared to a servant who has fled from his master. He meets up with a friend who informs him that his master has sent messengers to seek him out. He then advises him, "When they find you, you will certainly be severely punished. However, I heard your master say that if you return before his messengers reveal your whereabouts he will not discipline you." The friend continues: "Listen to me. Return immediately and I will testify that I found you crying in remorse at having abandoned your post. Just hurry before the messengers reveal your hiding place."

The master is Hashem and Eliyahu the prophet is His messenger. When Eliyahu arrives we will have to deal with the repercussions of our sins. The time to return is now when we can do teshuvah the right way and spare ourselves unnecessary anguish. (*Zechor Le'Miriam* 4)

Food For Thought

Practically speaking it is a good idea to repent promptly for you may forget the sin and thus never repent. That is why we are urged to "throw off all our sins" (*Yechezkel* 18) so that we rid ourselves of spiritual impurity. The Chofetz Chaim compares this to a delivery man hired to lug a heavy package to a specific destination. As soon as he arrives, he immediately drops his heavy load. He is unwilling to carry it on his shoulder for an extra moment. The contamination resulting from our sins are in the same category as that onerous burden.

When a person commits a sin once and then a second time, it becomes permissible to him (*Kiddushin* 40a). He no longer views the sin with the same stringency. He has committed the sin twice and as far as he can see, he is the same person as before. It then becomes difficult for this person to experience proper regret for a sin that he no longer sees as terribly severe. He is now much more likely to repeat the offense again. (Reb Itzele Peterberger) He psychologically justifies his deed so that others who avoid what he now deems acceptable are judged as extreme. Of course he views his defiance as perfectly balanced.

There are some sins that are so "insignificant" that they barely generate a blip on the radar screen showing our service of Hashem. However when an "insignificant" sin consistently recurs, it moves into the category of a large sin. It is vital that we avoid repetition of a sin, even if it is a minor infraction. This type of repetition profanes the Name of Hashem, as it is an indication that we are unconcerned about Hashem's commands. (*Machaneh Yisroel, Teshuvah*) The Chofetz Chaim offers the following parable to elucidate the impact of repeated sin.

> *A talented florist fashioned exquisite bouquets which were a feast for the senses — beautiful to behold and with heavenly perfume. No wonder his store was always full of customers so that he made a very good living — and what a living! He loved every aspect of his work. Arranging the flowers was an outlet for his creativity and he luxuriated in the intoxicating fragrances in his store. The scents wafting*

out to the street were so enticing that visitors would enter just to indulge their senses and inevitably they would make some purchase.

One day when he arrived to open his store, he saw that a tannery had opened down the block. The odors emanating from that concern were so overpowering he nearly fainted. He immediately understood that this new neighbor would detrimentally affect his business. The proof was soon in coming. He was forced to close his front door to keep the horrible odor from invading his premises. From his plate-glass storefront, he noticed that many potential customers simply turned away before entering the block and chose another route. People held their nose as they hurried by. Seeing his front door closed, many fled without even knocking. He sat alone with his wilting flowers. Soon he was forced to hang a sign that read, "For Sale."

The next day, the door of the store was opened by his new neighbor wearing his dirty apron and bringing his trade's pungent smell in his wake. He scanned the store, noting the empty baskets of flowers and the forsaken wrapping paper. He began, "You have a nice place here. I have a proposal to make. Permit me to expand my operations into your premises and you will become my partner."

The florist found it difficult to respond. The proposal took him by surprise, plus it was difficult to think while taking shallow breaths to avoid inhaling through his nose.

"I will think about it," he answered politely, while thinking, "What an absurd proposal." His only wish was to get as far away from the tannery as possible. He was determined to sell his store and reopen in an environment with uncontaminated air. Yet the days passed and no buyer was forthcoming. His debts piled up and hunger loomed. He took a deep breath, knocked on the tannery door, and agreed. It wasn't long before the smells and the sounds of the tannery were emanating from the former florist's door.

The ex-florist donned an apron, rolled up his sleeves, and began mixing the lime. The first day, he breathed only through his mouth. Once he accidentally took a whiff of the environment and nearly passed out from intense nausea. The tanner simply said, as he revived him, "You'll get used to it."

He was right. The second day was better. The third day, he found the discomfort easing. The fourth and fifth day, it was starting not to bother him at all, and soon he was breathing normally.

At home, his wife welcomed the nice money he was earning. She was even able to put away some funds for a rainy day. After a while she told her husband that it was time for him to leave the tannery and open a store elsewhere.

"A store?" he asked puzzled. "What kind of a store."

"A florist, of course," she replied, surprised by his dimwittedness.

"Flowers," he snorted." I cannot tolerate the

spiritless people who can't breathe plain air and require the indulgence of flowers to perfume their environment...."

The Chofetz Chaim concludes that this is the meaning of the verse: "Do not contaminate yourselves through them lest you become contaminated through them" (*Vayikra* 11:43). Don't indulge in sin for it will attach itself to you and it will become second nature (*Mayan Ha'moed*, pg. 202–203). A sin loses its sting once one indulges in it. After he has wallowed in the mud, the dirt is no longer repulsive (Alter of Kelm).

Another dramatic ramification of repeating a transgression is the fact that even if he ultimately decides not to sin, his sinful thought is considered the equivalent of an action. Rashi explains that when a person consistently repeats a sin (without doing teshuvah in between) his refraining from sinning is not deemed to be for the sake of Heaven, but rather because he did not feel like committing the deed (*Rashi, Kiddushin* 40a)

Divine wrath and retribution will progressively increase toward one who is cognizant of his misdeeds but makes no use of the gift of teshuvah. Rabbeinu Yonah likens it to a band of robbers imprisoned by the king who manage to dig a tunnel for their escape. All flee except for one. When the prison warden discovers the tunnel and sees that one man has stayed behind, he begins to beat him with his stick. "Hapless one!" he screams. "The tunnel was open in front of you! Why did you not save yourself?" (*Koheles Rabbah* 7:32; *Shaarei Teshuvah* 1)

All that was needed was for him to crawl through the tunnel and he would have escaped. His inaction conveys more than mere foolishness. The fact that he did not make use of a golden opportunity to escape indicates that he is unafraid of the impending judgment against him.

When urging prompt teshuvah, Reb Itzele Peterburger writes that it stands to reason that since we are judged on *Rosh Ha'shanah* in single file as we pass before Hashem, those who go through early will get preferential treatment.

> ### Food For Thought
> Sluggishness and apathy in the realm of teshuvah is a terrible sin.
> (Chasam Sofer)

Because forgiveness is a *chessed*, it behooves us to repent quickly for one never knows if it will always be accessible. Prompt repentance forestalls punishment as it did for Bilaam, who confessed to sinning so that he would not be harmed by the angel (*Bamidbar Rabbah* 20:13).

> *A father went on a shopping trip, returning with a splendid new suit for his son. The boy proudly put it on and ran to show it off to his friends. A jealous acquaintance spitefully pushed him into the mud. His splendid new suit was now blotched. The boys gleefully ran to the boy's home to tell his father the sorry fate of his expensive purchase. But the boy, being a smart lad, sprinted ahead of them and burst*

into his home, crying pitifully, "My beautiful suit was ruined. I am so sorry."

The father felt sorry for his forlorn, mud-spattered son and assured him that his suit would be cleaned or he would buy him another one. By the time the other rascals reached the boy's home, they found the father drying his son's tears and saw that all was well between them.

When the news of wrongdoing is delivered by the the remorseful person responsible for the deed, it sounds very different than the *yetzer hara*'s revelation of the gory details. (Dubno Maggid)

Beginning the Teshuvah Process

Teshuvah begins with recognition of our self-worth and talents, as well as the greatness and importance of our forefathers and their preciousness to Hashem (Rabbeinu Yonah). When the soul is hewn from beneath the Heavenly Throne, it is imbued with the desire to return to its Source through the performance of good deeds. The body attempts to confuse the soul and distract it from its goals. Our job is to guide this longing in the right direction. In other words, the goal of our entire life is the process of return to our Source. The person who sins repeatedly makes the journey more arduous. But even if one sins only occasionally, one is still taken up by this process. (*Dibros Tzvi*, based on the *Ramchal*, pg. 188)

Ideally a person should repent for his evil ways while he is still strong and vigorous and capable of overcoming the evil inclination and doing a proper teshuvah.

Beginning the Teshuvah Process

> ## Food For Thought
> A *baal teshuvah* has to be strong as a lion to stand up to those who make fun of him.
>
> (Gra, *Mishlei* 31)

There was once a bank manager who suddenly decided to do teshuvah. He got up one morning and put on tefillin, davened, and said the berachos *on his breakfast. He then left for work as usual. In his office, his secretary brought him a cup of coffee and Danish as she did every day. He did not know how to proceed. He was determined not to eat without a* berachah, *but he would have to don his yarmulke to say the* berachah *and if he were to put it on and utter the blessing, his secretary would surely laugh heartily and he would be the talk of the bank. He would have happily refused the snack, but that would have aroused unwanted and unanswerable questions as well.*

Just then a good customer walked into his office with a heavy sack. Suddenly the sack tore and the gold coins inside scattered. The manger locked the door to the room and he and the secretary helped the rich man collect his scattered coins. The rich man crawled along the ground under the table and chairs gathering the coins with not the least bit of concern for his expensive clothing that was getting dirty and wrinkled and with no thought of his prominent standing in the community. The secretary did not laugh; she did not even smile as she crawled along picking up one coin after another. She felt bad about what had happened and eagerly lent a helping hand in the hope that the bank's client would recover all the coins.

The manager took in the scene and applied it to himself. Why is no one laughing at the rich man crawling on all fours making a fool of himself for some money? It is because they value gold and feel that there is nothing to be ashamed of in lowering oneself for money. If I want to say a berachah, *certainly it has no less value than the gold scattered on the floor. He decided to put on his yarmulke and say a* berachah *even if it would cause a lot of raised eyebrows. He would deal with the comments until everyone got used to the changes. That is exactly what he did. He took his now-cold coffee and Danish and said a* berachah *loud and clear. He did not neglect the* berachos *said after eating. Yes, there were snickers and even some outright laughter, but after a couple of days, his teshuvah was no longer of interest to anyone.*

(*Ohr Le'tziyon*, pg. 184–185)

Many have no idea where to begin. One thing is certain; a resolution to turn your life around is inadequate (without actions). The key to successful teshuvah is the sincere and honest desire to return to Hashem and the recognition of the joy that actualizing our potential brings in its wake. One should begin by recalling all the good that Hashem has done for him from his birth until the present day and how careful we ought to be not to return evil for good with our transgressions. (*Orchos Tzaddikim, Orchos Teshuvah*)

Teshuvah begins with the recognition that the person has lost something very precious — lost the connection between himself and Hashem. To regain this precious connection a person will have to examine his actions and identify those areas where the connection is weakest and in danger of coming loose. Next he needs to understand the causes of the breakdown of this connection, through an analysis of his actions, words, thoughts, and emotions to decide whether or not they are completely in accordance with Torah. The verse in *Eicha* (3:40), "Let us search and examine our ways and return to Hashem," describes the process.

Having completed this analysis, the *baal teshuvah* must incorporate this knowledge into his consciousness. He must then zero in on his weak points, use his strengths, and "return" to his previous state of spiritual purity. In the process, we restore our connection with the Almighty as well. This is what we truly want and we should be ready to do whatever is needed to attain this goal.

> **Food For Thought**
>
> Philosophers have grappled with the question of whether we exist. The Kotzker Rebbe answered the question by pointing out that a person's feelings of sincere repentance are an indication that he is definitely not living in a world of delusion.
>
> (*Emes Me'kotzk Titzmach*, pg. 60)

Because doing teshuvah can be hard work, inertia often prevents a person from starting the teshuvah process. When attempting to do teshuvah people are often overwhelmed by their many sins. It is important to note that making changes in behavior and fighting the negative tendencies which draw a person to sin are part of the challenges of life. The deciding factor in our ultimate success will be the desire to rise to the challenge and prevail despite it all. Rav Chaim Volozhiner offers the reassurance that as soon as a person concludes that he must repent, his resolution forges spiritual powers that assist the person to carry on (*Nefesh Chaim* 1:12).

One may feel that he lacks the power to refrain from sin if faced with temptation, even at the moment of teshuvah. Still, he honestly hopes not to sin again, he prays to avoid the test, and he is prepared to run from temptation. There are a number of factors that can make it very difficult to begin. They may include a sense of futility that follows from the extent of the lifestyle changes necessary to do complete teshuvah; the fear that the person's transgressions cannot or will not be forgiven; the fear of repetition should there be a test; concern with negative reactions from friends and family, of being misunderstood. A person doesn't need to have all the answers right now, and does not need to make every change at once. The key is the commitment to change.

> **INSPIRATION**
>
> "We must strengthen ourselves with good desires and yearnings, and we must be extremely determined, stubborn in fact, in our will. Each person must believe in himself; he must believe that the good that is in him is still very, very strong. 'Although I have done wrong,' he should say, 'still great waters cannot extinguish the love, and rivers cannot wash away [*Shir Ha'shirim* 8:7] the points of good that I have merited to grasp within this passing shadow that is life.'"
>
> (*Letters of Reb Nosson* #320)

Be aware of situations in which you're likely to stumble, and keep a safe distance from them. Build fences to protect yourself and resolve to strengthen yourself in the future. Just as one who is beginning to recover from an illness must guard himself against many things so as not to suffer a relapse, so one who is sick with transgression must guard himself exceedingly when he begins to repent. (*Orchos Tzaddikim, Teshuvah*)

The teshuvah process can be expedited by the study of the basic texts of teshuvah: *Shaarei Teshuvah*, by Rabbeinu Yonah, and *Hilchos Teshuvah* of the Rambam. Other useful texts are *Chovos Ha'levavos*, *Reishis Chochmah*, and *Beis Elokim*. Torah scholars and Rebbetzins can often provide sound practical advice for those who wish additional guidance.

The Alter of Novardok compared the situation to someone whose home was robbed. Thieves broke the lock on the front door to gain entry to the house. The owner of the house will certainly not continue to use the same lock. He will surely acquire a stronger lock, one that will make it far more difficult for burglars to pick and gain entry. (*Tenuas Ha'mussar*, vol. 4, pg. 307)

The teshuvah process involves a willing break with former, perhaps-ego-enhancing conduct, therefore it needs to include mitzvos that build a person's self-image. As with all other spiritual endeavors the balance must be maintained. The *Menoras Ha'maor* points out that visiting the sick and taking the time to pay our respects at the cemetery heightens our perception of the fragility of life and aids in the teshuvah process (Candle 5, section 1, ch. 2, *perek* 1).

Change Must Be Gradual

One can change but the change must be gradual. A person cannot ascend to the top rung of a ladder without first placing his foot on the bottom rung, but a person should not be satisfied by remaining on that rung. It is therefore not considered an infraction on the part of a servant if when commanded by his master to ascend a ladder; he begins by stepping on the bottom rung. However, if the servant refuses to move from his place and ascend upward, but instead goes back and forth from the floor to the bottom rung, then he is defying his master. (*Ruach Chaim* 1:13)

If you attempt to tackle too many things at once you will probably not get too far. Rabbi Pam recommends starting teshuvah in the areas you find naturally fulfilling. If you love doing *chessed*, you should seek to improve and increase your efforts in that area. If a person finds his davening spiritually elevating, he should increase the quantity and quality of his devotions. Even if a prospective *baal teshuvah* is involved in the commission of a number of serious *aveiros*, he should begin the teshuvah process with one step and continue one step at a time.

> *A student once cried to Rav Yechezkel Levenstein that he had sinned and was unable to do teshuvah and change his evil ways. Rabbi Yechezkel advised him not to despair. He assured the student that he would succeed by beginning with just one small step and that help from Hashem would surely follow.*
> (*Sichos Maamar Mordechai*, vol. 1, pg. 87)

It is vital that the teshuvah process be broken up into small manageable components. In a *Shabbos Shuva* lecture, the Rebbe Reb Shmelke of Nikolsburg offered the following analogy:

> *A man set out for the neighboring city on a sweltering summer day. The sun's rays were intense and the humidity made it agonizingly hot. Only a man with an iron will could carry on under such adverse conditions. What did he do? He said to himself, "Forget about walking to the next city. I will only walk to that tree up ahead." When he arrived at that tree, he said to himself, "I will continue walking to that house down the hill." This is the only way he could proceed from point to point and ultimately arrive at his destination.*

What you need to do is to tell yourself, "Just this one time, I'll do it," or "Only for a short time." This will help you to not feel overwhelmed. (*Michtav MeEliyahu*, vol. 3, pg. 293)

Choose small things or the easy parts of mitzvos to work on. An example of a resolution taken on by Rav Shach was to say the first *berachah* of *Bircas Ha'mazon* with *kavanah*. Rav Itzele Peterburger resolved to meditate before reciting a *berachah*. Rav Chaim Ozer Grodzinsky undertook to study a *mussar sefer* every day. Better to succeed in small things than to fail in big things. Even a small change for the better will enable us to start the process of teshuvah.

Putting your resolutions into writing and referring to them all year long to determine if you are sticking to them is one way of maintaining a stage of teshuvah all year long. Take one particular statement that really moves you and repeat it to yourself over and over again. When you continually think about something, those thoughts will have a strong effect. (*Michtav MeEliyahu*, vol. 1, pg. 260–261) Choose a new stirring statement periodically, to maintain its effectiveness. A number of small improvements add to massive self-control. They increase self-confidence and create a positive momentum. Taking upon oneself to strengthen one's observance of something small is symbolic of one's desire to improve in all areas. Knowing our limitations, we zero in on a commitment that we are likely to be able to keep.

When doing teshuvah one should always attempt to seek a rectification that duplicates the deed in a positive fashion. This concept is referred to as *"teshuvas ha'mishkal."* As an example, if a person reached erroneous conclusions in his service of Hashem because he was not conscientious enough to take the time for a lengthy thought process, he might consider taking upon himself not to occupy his mind with mundane matters. Another possibility would be to not allow himself to make precipitous, "instantaneous" decisions. If he sinned to please his body, he should repent by depriving his body. (*Moreh Nevuchim* 386) If he has run to perform a sin, he should now run to do a mitzvah. (*Zayis Raanan* by the *Magen Avrohom*)

Teshuvah helps for sins. But what about the mitzvos that were done improperly without the proper *kavanah*? To restore to good health, the angels that are crippled by insincerity undertake more heightened observance of certain mitzvos.

A person should be careful not to squander his spiritual arousal on unsuitable choices. Rav Eliyahu Lopian used to complain abut this trend. He would cite the example of a young man who might decide to start being careful abut false weights and measures.

"He's a fool," Rav Lopian would exclaim. "This young man never had and never will have anything to do with false measurements. He has no store and sells no merchandise. He must take upon himself something that's applicable to him." (Told by his *talmid*, Rabbi Moshe Aharon Stern, *mashgiach* of Kamenitz)

The *yetzer hara* enjoys helping a person trivialize observance by encouraging him to be meticulous about small matters to the point of foolishness; for example, picking up insignificant non-threatening objects from the street lest someone trip. In addition, a great deal of energy is wasted waging war against imaginary demons. Instead, a person should use his positive attributes to dispel the darkness. As the *Baal Ha'tanya* said, "We need not fight darkness with sticks. We need only strike a light." With good deeds a person can bring light into his life. Even a small show of self-control will get the demons off his back.

> *An elderly chassid once went to the Beis Yisroel to ask for guidance and a* berachah. *He described his spiritual condition, emphasizing his many shortcomings in all areas of Hashem's service. After detailing his failings in his study of Torah, davening,* middos, *and fear of Hashem, the chassid concluded, "If I make a spiritual reckoning and take stock of my situation, I realize that I have nothing!"*
>
> *The Beis Yisroel quickly retorted, "To realize you have nothing you don't need a* cheshbon *[calculation]. You could have concluded that without much reckoning. But if you make a true* cheshbon, *you will realize that you really have something and must strive for more!"*

Exercise

The Rambam suggests that we ought to visualize our ideal self, and then formulate specific steps for how to get from here to there. Many great people kept a notebook diary to further their self-knowledge. We can become wonderful people by acquiring the ability to communicate with ourselves.

The First Components of Teshuvah: Regret

Teshuvah encompasses one deed as well as embracing the action of one's entire lifetime. The process of thorough teshuvah can be very complex. All-inclusive repentance ranges from three steps to twenty. Below are the four most commonly held components of teshuvah.

Step 1 – Regret. Realize the extent of the damage and feel sincere regret.

Step 2 – Abandonment of Sin. Immediately stop the harmful action.

Step 3 – Confession. Articulate the mistake and ask for forgiveness.

Step 4 – Resolution. Make a firm commitment not to repeat it in the future.

Regret

It is not easy for a person to embrace the truth, because many illusions, stimuli, and habits vie for control of his psyche. It is difficult to free oneself from the shackles that encumber the spirit. Even when a person is convinced that he must change, the actualization of that change is a challenge. Like a bonded slave he cries out, "I love my master." (*Shemos* 21:5) His master is his ego, which has assumed control of his deeds. He must now take control of the flow of his thoughts and become master of his deeds and turn his focus to teshuvah. (Rav Chaim Ephraim Zaitchik)

The sooner a person admits his sins the better. No one can advance spiritually until he recognizes and admits his faults. The *Gemara* relates that Rav Yehoshua ben Chananya saw a captive child in prison and cited the verse, "Who made the house of Yaakov prey?"

The child replied, "Is this not because of Hashem, against Who we have sinned?" Rav Yehoshua ben Chananya declared, "I am sure this child will become a great rabbi."

What made him so certain? After all, the child had simply completed the verse. The Brisker Rav explains that after the destruction of the Beis Ha'mikdash many sought to lay the blame on everything and everyone but themselves. Rav Chananya perceived that the child's quality of admitting the truth would eventually lead him to greatness. (*Tranquility in the Home*, Rabbi Moshe Aharon Stern, pg. 208–209)

Food For Thought

The Jews were forgiven for the Sin of the Golden Calf because they fully admitted their guilt. This was unlike the Sin of the Spies, where they did not readily perceive their error and acknowledge their guilt.

It is usually excruciatingly difficult for us to admit that we have done wrong. We tend to excuse ourselves. We refuse to admit the truth. We shift blame to others. We excel at rationalizing. But the person who wrenches from himself the unpleasant truth, "I have sinned," has performed a great and meaningful act.

> ### Inspiration
>
> The Kotzker Rebbe asks why a person must bring a more expensive sacrifice when he is uncertain as to whether he sinned. He explains that a person who knows he has sinned has already partially repented. The person who has not acknowledged his sin is a long way from repentance and therefore requires a more significant sacrifice.
>
> (*Emes Me'kotzk Titzmach* #167, pg. 60)

We try to justify our actions, using a variety of excuses:
- "Everyone is doing it"
- "At least I'm not like some people who go around stealing and hurting people!"
- "Who are *you* to say it's wrong?!"
- "I'm really a good person. I just don't think we need to do [whatever it is]."

That is why this first step of teshuvah is indeed the most crucial — and can be the most difficult. Unless a person feels regret, he will most likely continue in his errant ways. If you are finding this step difficult, vis a vis a few sins, then consider the examples of *baalei teshuvah*. At one point they acknowledge that almost everything they thought, said, did, aspired to — almost all their lives — was mistaken. They admit this and proceed to change the entire course of their life.

> ### Food For Thought
> Reb Itzele Peterberger said, "A person who regrets his sin is recorded Above as having sinned and later bemoaned his sin. A person who is not remorseful is recorded Above as having sinned and not regretted his sin. The distance between the two recorded incidents is like the distance between heaven and earth even though they both refer to an identical deed.
> (*Shuvah Yisroel*, pg. 196)

In essence, every sin is a barrier between us and Hashem. One forbidden action, inappropriate word, or a show of anger or other negative trait, causes one separate barrier. A thousand such errors cause a thousand such barriers. How many have we erected over the past year? How can one not feel remorse about the distance from his Creator that he has caused himself? To feel ashamed of something is to distance oneself from it in contrast to the insolent person who identifies with his sin.

Teshuvah must include deep remorse. Remorse begins with pondering the gravity of sin until this reality penetrates deep into the heart. Having concluded that sin is something from which a person must refrain, one is ready to proceed with an honest self-evaluation that opens the eyes of the mind and causes a profound sense of embarrassment. A person should say in his heart, "What have I done? How could the awe of Hashem not have been before my eyes? How could I have not feared the repercussions of my transgression? How could I have not subdued my evil inclination for a momentary pleasure? How could I have sullied my pure soul, which was breathed into me by the Source of Holiness? How could I have traded away a great, eternally enduring world for a small, ephemeral world? How could I not have remembered the day of death, which will leave before my soul only my corpse and my dust?" (*Orchos Tzaddikim, Shaar Teshuvah*)

A regretful person is most certainly embittered by each individual sin he committed and is deeply distressed about how he could ever have thought to behave in a way that is contrary to the will of Hashem, who generously gives life. He asks himself, "How could I have acted so foolishly? How could I have been so blind and foolish before the Almighty, the Omnipresent, 'Who in His goodness renews each day, continuously, the work of Creation?' How could I have forsaken the Ultimate, the Absolute, for some transient illusion?" As the prophet laments: "My people have committed two evils: they have forsaken Me, the Fountain of Living Waters, to hew for themselves cisterns, broken cisterns that hold no water!" (*Yirmiyahu* 2:13)

Rabbeinu Yonah eloquently describes the agonizing process of regretting sin: "Ponder the wickedness of one who defers repentance, for it is great. If he would not delay, but would repent immediately, sighing in bitterness of heart, in agitation and anxiety, his eyes overflowing in sorrow, then, when his evil inclination would encounter him a second time and set sin before him, he would conquer his inclination. He would recall his experience with the cup of bitterness and would not drink from it again. As it is written: 'Be agitated and do no sin,' meaning, become agitated and pained that you sinned and sin no more.... This interpretation is borne out by the verses 'Do not become agitated on the way' [*Bereishis* 45:24] and 'I grow agitated where I stand' [*Chavakuk* 3:16]. This agitation signifies extreme remorse over the past and the present. It is precisely for this reason that the word [agitated] was chosen here, as opposed to fear or cowering." (Rabbeinu Yonah)

> *In his youth, the famed Maggid of Zlotchov, Rabbi Yechiel Michel, lived in a certain town, where he would sit all day in the local* beis medrash *and study.*
>
> *In that town lived a simple Jew who earned his livelihood by transporting travelers and merchandise in his wagon. One day, the wagon driver came to the local rabbi, greatly distressed. "Help me, Rabbi!" he wept. "I have committed a terrible sin. I have desecrated the holy Shabbos. How can I atone for my transgression?"*
>
> *"How did this come to pass?" asked the rabbi.*
>
> *"Last Friday," the man explained, "I was returning from the marketplace with a wagonload of*

merchandise when I lost my way in the forest. By the time I found my way to the outskirts of the city, the sun had already set. So preoccupied was I with my worry over the merchandise that I failed to realize that the Shabbos had arrived until it was too late...."

Seeing how brokenhearted the man was, the rabbi comforted him and said: "My son, the Gates of Repentance are never closed. Donate a box of candles to the synagogue and your transgression will be forgiven."

The young prodigy, Reb Michel, overheard this exchange, and was displeased by the rabbi's approach. "A box of candles to atone for violating the Shabbos?" he thought. "The Shabbos is one of the most important mitzvos of the Torah! Why is the rabbi treating the matter so lightly?"

That Friday afternoon, the wagon driver brought the candles to the synagogue. As Reb Michel watched disapprovingly from his table against the back wall, the driver placed them on the lectern for the shammes to light in honor of the Shabbos. But this was not to be. Before the shammes arrived, a stray dog carried off the candles and ate them.

The distraught penitent ran to report the incident to the rabbi. "Woe is me!" he wept. "My repentance has been rejected in Heaven! What shall I do?!"

"You're making too much of the matter," the rabbi reassured him. "These things happen — there's no reason to deduce that Hashem is rejecting your repentance. Bring another box of candles to the synagogue next week, and everything will be all right."

But when the shammes lit the candles on the following Friday afternoon, they inexplicably melted down, so that by the time Shabbos began, nothing was left of them. On his third attempt, the week after that, a strong wind suddenly blew out the candles, just when Shabbos began, and it was not possible to relight them.

The rabbi, too, realized, that something was amiss, and advised the wagon driver to seek the counsel of Rabbi Yisroel Baal Shem Tov.

Said the Baal Shem Tov, upon hearing the man's story, "It seems that a certain young scholar in your town finds fault with the path to repentance that the rabbi has prescribed for you. Never mind. Next week, donate another box of candles to the synagogue. This time, I promise you that everything will be all right. And tell Reb Michel that I would be honored if he could trouble himself to come visit me."

Reb Michel wasted no time in abiding by the Baal Shem Tov's request. But as soon as he and his coachman set out, all sorts of troubles beset their journey. First, the wagon tumbled into a ditch. Then, an axle broke many miles from the nearest town. After that, they lost their way altogether. When they finally found the road to Mezibuzh it was late Friday afternoon and the sun was about to set. They were forced to abandon the wagon and continue on foot.

Reb Michel arrived at the Baal Shem Tov's door an hour into Shabbos, weary and traumatized by his near-violation of the holy day. "Good Shabbos,

Reb Michel," Reb Israel greeted him. "Come in and warm yourself by the fire. You, Reb Michel, have never tasted sin, so you did not comprehend the remorse a Jew feels at having transgressed the will of his Father in Heaven. I trust that you now understand something of the agony that our friend the wagon driver experienced and that you now value his teshuvah. Believe me, his remorse alone more than atoned for his unwitting transgression...."

(Rabbi Y.S. Zevin, *Sippurei Chassidim: Chassidic Tales*)

Remember that Hashem takes note of man's every deed and exacts retribution in accordance with the wickedness of his ways. Ponder the reckoning and retribution that we will have to face for every sin committed. The spiritual damage is enormous. Rabbeinu Yonah writes: "One should perceive in his heart that to forsake Hashem is wicked and bitter and he should take to heart that there is punishment meted out for each sin" (*Shaarei Teshuvah* 1:10).

Regret includes the positive acknowledgement that while my essence remains uncorrupted, I have failed to live up to my potential. When a person experiences this type of anguish he is eager for a remedy. To use this shame in a constructive manner, a person at the moment of trial should try to visualize the loss incurred by succumbing to the *yetzer hara* versus the inestimable achievement of controlling his desires. If he succeeds, he will quite likely refrain from sinning. This first step in the process of repentance is not a negative thought process but rather a positive constructive tool.

It enables the person to cut himself off from destructive tendencies in his past and latch on to channels of Heavenly assistance which will enable the contrite person to recreate himself in a new image. (*Hegyonos*)

It is useful to make a list of our sins, to expedite the process of repentance (*Chovos Ha'levavos, Shaar Prishus* 5; *Sefer Chassidim* 201). This list helps us fulfill the dictum that our sin should be before us always (*Hisragshus Ha'lev* 2:5). Studying the third *shaar* of Rabbeinu Yonah is also very helpful. Rabbi Yisroel Salanter advised that a person spend additional time analyzing the sections of *Shaarei Teshuvah* that are most relevant to him personally. (*Ohr Yisroel*, Letter 7)

He who is not bothered by his actions and sees no reason to discontinue his wayward deeds is far from performing teshuvah. The severity of such a condition is so great that *Chazal* declare that he who is far from teshuvah has possibly forfeited his portion in the World to Come. (See *Shaarei Teshuvah* 3:141)

Food For Thought

"If one commits a sin and is ashamed of it, his sin is forgiven. Moreover, if he merely considers the idea of penitence he is already counted among the penitents and elevated to the Throne of Glory…. he is immediately elevated to the highest of heavens, not to the first but to the seventh, and he is not left there but brought unto the Throne of Glory."

(*Vayikra Rabbah* 30)

One Rosh Ha'shanah, the Sar Shalom of Belz sent his son to listen in on the conversation of two chassidim. The boy reported back to his father that one chassid said, "Oy, today is Rosh Ha'shanah — an awesome, terrifying day. What are we setting before the Creator of the world, Who examines our thoughts and deeds?" His friend responded by sighing from the depth of his heart as thoughts of teshuvah shrouded him in anxiety.

The Rebbe explained to his son that this conversation had a great impact in Heaven. The accusing angels had claimed that non-Jews were also charitable and also did many good deeds. The defense embraced the conversation of the two men as it rose to Heaven and presented it to the accusing angels, crying, "There is one thing that non-Jews definitely don't have, and that is a broken heart! The accusing angel had to agree that only Jews are truly anguished at their sins.

(*Kisvei Chassidim*)

Food For Thought

Rabbi Menachem Mendel of Lubavitch, the Tzemach Tzedek, said, "One with a good imagination achieves repentance more easily."

(*Likutei Dibburim*, vol. 1, pg. 157)

"If a man loses a *dinar*, it is distressing to him, and if he loses all of his wealth he mourns and his heart is bitter within him. And much more so should one be aggrieved for having rebelled against Hashem and having corrupted his way before Him" (*Orchos Tzaddikim, Teshuvah*).

Imagine someone throwing a piece of paper into a fire, only to realize minutes later that the paper was actually a document worth thousands of dollars. The regret and mental anguish that this person would experience is the sort of regret a Jew should experience on doing that which is contrary to Hashem's will.

> Someone once came to the Belzer Rebbe, Reb Yissochar Dov, to ask for help in doing teshuvah. "How much do I have to regret my deeds?" "I'll tell you a story," the Rebbe said, and told him the following parable: A merchant with several wagons laden with goods, arrived early at the Leipzig fair. That day it rained heavily; all the other merchants remained stuck on the road. Because the other merchants had not yet arrived, the buyers besieged the "early bird," who decided to hold off in the expectation of better offers. As he had no competitor, he was already relishing the small fortune he was about to make. But the next morning the sun came out. Before the merchant had clinched a deal, the other merchants began arriving. Consider his anguish at his lost opportunity. He could have made so much money and now he lost everything.

The Second Component of Teshuvah: Abandonment of Sin

According to the Alter Rebbe, abandonment of the sin includes resolving not to transgress any mitzvos in the future while accepting upon oneself the yoke of Hashem's Kingship. This atones for having thrown off the yoke of Heaven and blemishing his soul. When one accepts upon oneself the yoke of Heaven, he corrects both the personal and cosmic weakness caused by the sin.

There are differences of opinion as to the order of teshuvah. We have placed regret before abandonment of sin. However there are circumstances where the order must be reversed.

A person who is so caught up in sin, to the point where he feels he won't be able to overcome the temptation the next time he encounters it, may benefit by first distancing himself from the sin so that he is removed from temptation. Sometimes a person's environment is responsible for his continued sins. For some people the only way to begin the process of repentance is first to uproot themselves from that place and renounce all corrupting influences.

Abandonment of Sin

When a person sins repeatedly his heart is wrapped in layer upon layer of contamination. Often his regret is incapable of penetrating these numerous layers. He cannot pierce the dense impurity engendered by his sins. Each abandonment of sin slackens the ropes that bind the sinner, thus enabling his mind to clear. He is then capable of moving to the level of regret required by the true penitent and throwing off the layers of corruption. (Rabbeinu Yonah, *Shaarei Teshuvah, Shaar Rishon*)

When a person is tempted to sin he must put up a fight and battle his *yetzer hara* tooth and nail. If, unfortunately, he is not successful, he should at least feel bad that he could not overcome the temptation. That way, in Heaven, the *aveira* will be recorded as one that was committed regretfully. Reb Itzele Peterburger said that the difference between one who sins with "a groan" and he who sins without "a groan" is tremendous. He should then dig in his heels with the determination not to succumb the next time around.

Food For Thought

Teshuvah is not an absolute, "winner take all" process. It is about searching out the bad, "taking what is good," and building on it, thus ensuring that we continue to forge forward in our struggle to become better Jews. Teshuvah is different from other mitzvos in that it can be partially fulfilled. Tzitzis require four sets of fringes, tefillin require

> four segments — three won't do for either. However, if a person does not fulfill all the aspects of teshuvah, there is still some atonement achieved. (*Beis Elokim, Shaar Teshuvah* 12) Even by simply renouncing his sin a person moves closer to Hashem. Each additional step of teshuvah brings him closer and closer.
>
> (Mishnas Reb Aharon)

The Mabit maintains that regret and cessation of sin are the most important segments of teshuvah. A sin involves thought and deed. Planning involves thought and actualization involves action. When a person experience regret in his mind, he atones for the planning stage. When he has the opportunity to sin again and does not do so or when he has the opportunity to do a mitzvah which he previously ignored and this time actually sees it through, he atones for the deed. (*Beis Elokim, Shaar Teshuvah* 2:103)

The Third Component of Teshuvah: Confession and Asking for Forgivness

Everyone who confesses will receive a portion in the World to Come (*Sanhedrin* 44). The Rambam cites repentance and confession as mitzvah number 365. When the person confesses, he ensures that the angels formed by his sins can no longer harm him (see commentaries on Bilaam's confrontation with his donkey in *Bamidbar* 22).

> ### Inspiration
>
> The etymology of the word "vidui" is "to throw," suggesting that the words of the Yom Kippur Vidui prayer should be thrown forth from the innermost recess of the heart and uttered with heartfelt kavanah (Rav Chaim Friedlander). They require great preparation, both in order to understand the words and to recognize the sin that one is confessing (Yesod Ve'shoresh Ha'avodah 11:11). One should consider well, beforehand, what it is that he is

> asking forgiveness for and commit himself not to return to that foolish sin (Chofetz Chaim, Appendix to Shem Olam). Ideally one should personalize the prayer of Vidui, citing his own personal examples (Ramah, Chayei Adam). Because it is a positive commandment, he should first say, "I am about to perform the positive commandment of Vidui" (Yesod Ve'shoresh Ha'avodah).

We must confess our mistakes out loud. Rav Nosson Tzvi Finkel would verbalize every step of teshuvah believing that the verbalization would have a greater impact on his psyche (*Ha'meoros Ha'gedolim* #76). Man has all sorts of thoughts flitting constantly through his mind. For his thoughts to have lasting meaning, he must express them in words. When two people don't get along, the first thing to do is to bring them together and get them to talk to each other. Then they can work out their differences. In the same way, we have been distanced from Hashem through our *aveiros*. Now that we are ready to come back, we must begin by talking to one another. (Rav Shimshon Pincus)

Inspiration

> After recording the rebuke of Nassan the prophet, there is a blank space in *Navi* before Dovid Ha'melech's response. The Vilna Gaon explains that the king could

have justified his deed, for technically he had not sinned (*Shabbos* 56a). He had the right to punish Uriah for his insolence and he knew that Batsheva was his intended queen (*Sanhedrin* 107a). He silently contemplated Nassan's words and finally make his decision. He replied, "I have sinned to Hashem." Nassan answered, "Then Hashem has removed your sin and you will not die." (*Samuel II* 12:1–12)

Unfortunately Adam did not confess immediately when confronted by Hashem. He tried to shift the blame to Chavah. If he had confessed he would not have been banished from *Gan Eden* and his sin would have been forgiven. (*Birchas Mayer*, pg. 87) According to the Sforno, Hashem's anger was aroused against Miriam and Aharon when they spoke out against their brother because they did not admit their sin immediately (*Bamidbar* 11). If King Shaul would have confessed immediately he would not have lost the kingdom (*Haskel Ve'yadoa Osi*, pg. 32) Because King Shaul did not confess his sin, he found that all Heavenly fountains of guidance were closed to him, as he himself told the prophet Shmuel when he summoned him for advice (*Igeres Ha'yediah*, pg. 225).

The *Midrash* asks, "How must one confess on *Yom Kippur*?" and answers, "He must state, 'I admit that I have been on a wayward path and I will not continue to do that which I have previously done. May it be Your will to forgive me for all my transgressions.' Rav Yitzchok says, 'This is comparable to someone who solders two poles together.' "

Rav Shlomo Wolbe explains this comparison as follows: Theoretically, the natural situation of a person is to be connected to Hashem. He is a *tzelem Elokim,* and just as a *"tzel"* (shadow) is connected to the object causing the shadow, so too the *"tzelem"* is connected to *Elokim.* Unfortunately by committing the *aveirah* he has "broken the rod into two," thereby obligating him to solder the pieces back together again. This is accomplished through *Vidui.* In the confession one states, "For the sin we have committed *before You.*" Prior to one's sin he stood "before Hashem" and after the fact he now stands at a distance. This, in turn, generates fiery feelings of remorse — the fire needed to solder the two rods back together again.

Inspiration

"By admitting out loud to the sin, the sinner renders his thoughts concrete. He makes it clear that he sincerely believes what he did is apparent to Hashem, and he will not treat Hashem's Eye which sees as one which does not see. Also, by stating the sin, especially when he regrets it, he will be careful about it the next time. It ensures that he will not fail again, after he has stated orally, "I have done the following and I was stupid in my actions."

(*Chinuch*)

If you recognize that you have sinned, then step into the Presence of Hashem and say, "O Hashem I have erred and sinned. I have been disobedient before You. I have done such-and-such. I am sorry and I am ashamed of what I have done and will never do it again" ... Feel in yourself how every sin you have committed, however small, even in the mind and heart, immediately brings with it a curse. Namely, that it makes you less capable of doing good, and further inclined to sin. When you have recognized this, then you can lay the future of your inner and outer life in the just and forgiving Hand of Hashem.

As you see yourself in spirit, so confess in word, in order that the picture of your self-abasement may become external to you and stand before you, making it not a passing emotion but a permanent mood and frame of mind which can bear fruit in practical conduct.

(*Horev* 514)

When confessing our sins it is customary to beat the chest just over the heart as a symbol of repentance as each transgression is enumerated. Yet logically the opposite would seem to make more sense: Should not the heart strike out at the hand that actually committed the sin? Our intention, however, is the source of all transgression — the lusts and desires of the heart that lead to sin.

> **Food For Thought**
>
> Referring to the practice of beating one's heart when reciting the confession of sins, the Chofetz Chaim explained: G-d does not forgive those who smite their heart, but He pardons those whose heart smites *them* for the sins they committed.

One of the sins we enumerate is: "For the sin that we have sinned with an insincere confession" (literally "a confession of the mouth"). This refers to the sin to which we have already confessed, but have only given lip service, as it states in *Tehillim*: "For my transgression I will tell; I am worried that I not sin." Although the lips may have declared their concern, the heart does not participate. (*Toras Yitzchok*) It is to this group that Hashem addresses the words "*shuvu banim shovivim.*" (Reb Zusha of Anipoli)

Rav Chaim Volozhiner got married in an inn along the highway. Unfortunately there was no Sefer Torah available for the wedding party to use for Kriyas HaTorah during sheva berachos. Rav Chaim wanted to set out in search of a Torah. However, an elderly Rav who was present insisted that it was not necessary. Rav Chaim suggested that a Sefer Torah be brought to them, but the elderly sage insisted that doing so was inappropriate. Because the opposition was so vehement, Rav Chaim fell silent and for the first time in his adult life he did not participate in a public reading of the Torah.

When he returned home after sheva berachos, he discovered that his private Sefer Torah had been stolen. He attributed the theft to the fact that he had missed the Torah reading that Monday. Heartbroken, he went to his room to reflect and repent. He was in the midst of his confession when someone came running in to tell him that the Torah was discovered.

A Russian soldier had been caught trying to sell the Torah, which was then returned to Rav Chaim. To the astonishment of those present, when the Sefer Torah was examined it was found that one section was missing. It was the section that Rav Chaim had missed out on hearing the week before.

Rav Chaim commented, "Look how wondrous are Hashem's reckonings. As soon as I did teshuvah, confessing my sin, my loss was restored in a way that brought home the deleterious effect of my offense."

(Avi Ha'yeshivos)

Food For Thought

A person should say *Vidui* with a humble heart, a bent head, and a choked up voice. If the *Vidui* is not a heartfelt confession, it is best not to say it at all.

(Peleh Yoetz)

A villager came to the big city for the first time, lodging at an inn. He was awakened in the middle of the night by the loud beating of drums and he inquired drowsily, "What's going on?" He was informed that a fire had broken out and that the drum beating was the city's fire alarm. He turned over and went back to sleep.

On his return home, he reported to the village authorities: "They have a wonderful system in the big city: when a fire breaks out the people beat their drums and before long the fire burns out." Excited, they ordered a supply of drums and distributed them to the population. When a fire broke out some time later, there was a deafening explosion of drum beating, and while the people waited expectantly for the flames to subside, a number of their homes burned to the ground.

A sophisticated visitor passing through that village, when told the reason for the ear-splitting din, derided these village simpletons: "Idiots! Do you think a fire can be put out by beating drums? They only sound an alarm for the people to wake up and take measures to extinguish the fire."

This parable, said the Maggid of Dubno, applies to those of us who believe that beating the breast during the Al Cheit *(confessional), raising our voices during worship, and blowing the shofar will extinguish the fires of sin and evil that burn in us. The confession must follow on the heels of the previous steps and be followed by the next one.*

true remorse, and of a break with the past. To achieve this level assures forgiveness. Of course, the shame must be true and deep. And naturally, the only One Who is able to evaluate this is the Judge of all the World, Who sees the innermost recesses of every heart.

> *During the time of the holy Ari, the wicked lived in terror. Whenever he saw them, the Ari would reveal to them every detail of the transgressions that each had committed over the past fifty years. And even if someone had merely contemplated sin in his heart, the Ari would reveal it. For this reason, the wicked would flee from him in shame, lest he gaze at them and reveal their guilt.*
> (*Emek Ha'melech*, Introduction to section III, 4:11b)

If this was the case in the presence of a mere human, how much greater will be the sinner's shame when he comes before the King of the Universe! Consider the following: you leave from your house one morning to find a camera crew camped at your doorstep. They inform you that you will be followed and filmed the entire day. Every move, every step, every word, and every thought of yours will be captured on film. At the end of the day you are given the record of all that has transpired. Imagine the joy at the sight of all the good deeds you performed. But imagine also the shame when you see the sins you committed that day. Now imagine having your friends and relatives watching with you. (*A Treasure for Life*, Rabbi A. Yachnes)

> ## Food For Thought
>
> *Teshuvah* is directly related to *bushah* (shame, embarrassment). The Hebrew word "*teshuvah*" contains the letters of "*boshes*"; transposing the letters of *shuvah* (return) offers the word *bushah* (shame). For *bushah* is a vital component of *teshuvah*.
>
> According to the *Orchos Tzaddikim*, "Understanding leads to shame and shame is a result of understanding."

> ## Food For Thought
>
> "Rabbi Bar-Chanina Sava said in the name of Rav, 'Anyone who does a sin and is ashamed of it, all his sins are forgiven!'"
>
> (*Berachos* 12b)

Rabbeinu Yonah graphically describes the shame of the soul standing before Hashem (see *Avos* 3): "Now imagine the mental activity of a disembodied soul, standing naked before Hashem. The 'volume control' is gone entirely. The mind is open and transparent. There is no jamming mechanism to diminish its force. Things can be perceived in a way that is impossible to a mind unencumbered by a body and a nervous system. You will remember everything you ever did and see it in a new light. You will see it in Hashem's own light that shines from one end of creation to the other. The memory of every good deed and mitzvah will be the most sublime of pleasures. The deeds of which we are ashamed cannot be rationalized away or dismissed. A person faces himself fully aware of the consequences of all his deeds. There will be no escape from the shame and no place to escape." (Adapted from *On Immortality and the Soul* by Rabbi Aryeh Kaplan.)

> ### INSPIRATION
>
> The Tiferes Shalom interprets the verse in *Devarim* (30:8), "You will return and hearken," as a reference to meriting ascending to higher levels of teshuvah, each of which will bring us to an even higher level.

Without a doubt, a man who has been hospitalized for an extended time, after having eaten a food that was harmful to his health, will be deterred from eating that food again, at least for a while. Similarly, the regret, sorrow, and soul-searching which are essential elements of teshuvah serve as a deterrent to future sin.

One has to be careful that the shame of failure does not result in sadness and disappointment in ourselves. This sadness has nothing to do with the mitzvah of teshuvah. Awareness of our failures should be linked with out knowledge that the area in which one is the weakest is the very area in which he is a vessel ready to receive Hashem's blessing. (*Tzidkas Ha'tzaddik* 181) It has been said in the name of the Gra that areas of resistance and failure are sometimes the only indication that this is the field of endeavor we have been sent to this world to rectify. This knowledge should rouse us to wage fierce war against our evil inclination in our desire to achieve perfection.

> *A distinguished person approached Rav Yisroel Salanter with a halachic query while he was in the midst of a lecture. After he finished speaking to the gentleman, he groaned. When he was asked why he had groaned, he replied, "When I was answering his question I was embarrassed by the fact that my sleeve was torn. After my initial reaction, I thought to myself that if a tear on my sleeve distressed me so much how much greater will my shame be in the* World to Come *as a result of the tear and stains on my soul if I do not correct them while there is still time."*
>
> (*Ha'meoros Ha'gedolim*)

We cannot expect to purify ourselves until we have completed the teshuvah process. A person who aspires to the ultimate in repentance must first cleanse himself of the filth of sin.

> *This can be compared to a rich man who saw a poor man — filthy, reeking, ragged, and unkempt — scrounging around in the garbage.*
> *The rich man's compassion was aroused and he*

made the poor man an offer. "I am ready to hire you as my servant. You will live with me and I will take care of your needs and pay you two gold dinars a week.

The poor man's eyes lit up. He ran to hug his benefactor. His new master wriggled out of his grip with a look of distaste. He said to his new servant, "Wait till we get to my house. You will bathe and I will supply you with new clothes. Then you will be ready to start your duties.

The poor man, duly chastened, maintained a proper distance while accompanying his new master home.

When they arrived he was escorted to the washroom where he removed his soiled clothing. A display of beautiful bottles caught his eye. Opening one after another he was enchanted by their wondrous fragrance. He immediately concluded that they were meant for him and began pouring them all over his unwashed body. Satisfied with the results, he put on the clean clothing that had been prepared for him and sought out his master. The malodorous blend of perfume and grime preceded his entry to the room. The rich man ran for the window, throwing it open for some fresh air. In a choked voice he shouted, "You have wasted my perfumes on your filth-encrusted body! First remove the grime and after that you can use my perfumes, if you wish!"

(Rav Avrohom Ha'kohein of Sfaks, Tunisia)

19
Teshuvah for Bad *Middos*

Bad character distorts our perspective so that we can no longer discern what is expected of us. The purer a person's character traits the more fine tuned his understanding of right and wrong. Doing teshuvah for bad character traits heals the illnesses of the soul. (*Shemoneh Perakim* of the Rambam)

Try to develop the skills that allow you to see the *middos* that drive our actions. Since all our deeds flow from our *middos*, it helps to ask ourselves regularly: "What is causing me to do this?"

If you are unclear as to which *middos* you have to work on, be alert as to what is difficult for you. If you find it difficult to lend any of your possessions, you might have to work on your *ahavas Yisroel* (love of your fellow Jew). If you absolutely can't keep a secret, then you might need to work on the *middah* of *shesika* (silence). If you tell too many self-protective lies, then you need to be scrupulously honest. If you are unable to focus on your davening, try to identify which character traits are interfering with your *kavanah*. Is it lack of discipline, lack of faith, conceit, or other character issues?

Pay careful attention to your thought, words, and actions. A journal is an invaluable tool towards self-knowledge. It is important that you identify your naturally strong character traits, for our strong *middos* will help us overcome the weaker *middos* within us. When you decide which character traits you should be working on, try zeroing in on the root causes. When do I fail like this? What is there in the environment? What else has happened today? Under which specific circumstances do I fail? What can I do to change those circumstances? In order to change, you must find specific techniques that are appropriate for your unique personality and situation. (*Toras Avrohom*, pg. 410) The Piasczner Rebbe points out that if you have not developed your own repertoire of techniques, it is an indication that you are not really trying to change. (*Bnei Machshava Tovah*)

Middos and habits generally have "triggers." For example, certain people provoke an angry, aggressive response. Other people may not pose a problem. The "trigger" might be specific activities, such as *Erev Shabbos* preparations, caring for fighting siblings, waiting in lines at government offices, and so on.

The same is true for other temptations. Laziness comes naturally when one is surrounded by various distractions, and most important, other lazy people. If we associate with the just and wise, it will be easier to upgrade our wisdom. The key is to control the environment by avoiding some things and creatively adding others so that it will be easier to do the right thing.

> **Food For Thought**
>
> It is hard to come close to Hashem if our soul lies asleep swathed in materialism. We must keep our soul alert by calling on it regularly when doing mitzvos. (*Chovos Ha'talmidim*) The best way to do so is to enthusiastically fulfill as many mitzvos as we can.

It is very beneficial to change our environment to avoid the triggers. (The most effective positive environment is doing mitzvos with other people: Learn in a *beis medrash*, visit the hospital *with others*, plan a *chessed* project *with others*, teach Torah *in a school*, etc.) Certain activities cause tension, which triggers anger. If you cannot avoid those activities, alternate them with relaxing activities.

A second solution is to *add* something to the environment which will make it easier to do the right thing. Join with a group or friend to work on *middos*. Attend a workshop which focuses on personal growth. If you have trouble getting up for davening in shul, take a study partner for ten minutes before davening. Then, when the alarm rings and you reach over to push the snooze button, you will think: "But what if my study partner comes and I'm not there?" The thought is so embarrassing it will get you up!

In many cases you can make a contract with yourself. Always keep in mind that you can not go against your nature completely, but you should channel it to a straight path.

(*Even Shlomo*) You might say to yourself, "If I succeed in overcoming the temptation (enough times) then I will allow myself something I very much enjoy." This is what is called a "behavior contract." Thus you have a personal incentive to do the right thing. For example: "If I get through the meeting without getting angry, I will allow myself to buy that picture for the wall/go to that restaurant/buy that expensive book, etc."

As long as the bad habits and *middos* are active, it is very difficult to gain control. Therefore, avoiding the triggers and adding payoffs may be the only way to gain control and ultimately become immune to the temptations. But this may require two stages: Trying to do without the first stage may make the second stage impossible. (Adapted from *Let's Face It* by Tzipporah Heller.) When working on your *middos* always remember that when you are feeling overwhelmed, it is time to move on.

Exercise

- Keep a personal list of sayings from our Sages that have a positive effect on your character development. Review it regularly. (*Chayei Ha'mussar II*, pg. 154)
- Publicizing your resolutions in the area of personal growth to friends and or relatives may help you keep your resolutions. (*Gateway to Self-Knowledge*, pg. 73)
- Avoiding the triggers of bad character and adding payoffs for self-control enables us to develop the psychological strength to deal with bad character.

Humility as an Aid to Teshuvah

The *Orchos Tzaddikim* and Rabbeinu Yonah consider humility to be one of the fundamentals of repentance. A haughty person loses sight of G-d and sins without hesitation. Indeed, pride is the cause of numerous sins. Man's evil deeds and the arrogance underlying them have built a barrier between Hashem and himself. That is why humility must be at the forefront of the teshuvah process. (*Chovos Ha'levavos*)

The Chofetz Chaim advises that a person keep his head lowered, looking at the ground where he will eventually end up. This is a compelling reminder that as he came from the earth, to the earth he will return. (*Nidchei Yisroel* 35:80)

It is difficult for someone who is an egotist to repent, for he will always find justifications for his evil behavior. Sometimes he attributes the fault to his environment or to his *yetzer hara*, thus ensuring that he remains blissfully free of responsibility. Such a person will never move beyond the first stage of repentance. Haughtiness prepares the background for a host of evil deeds. A sin will always contain an element of "I don't care" at its heart. A humble person will find it difficult to do something he wants to do when it conflicts with what Hashem wants.

We must model our prayers during Elul on those of Moshe Rabbeinu begging for forgiveness on behalf of his errant people. Such prayer was certainly heavily seasoned with humility. The prayer of a contrite person is on a higher plane than that of a person who is free of sin. (*Divrei Moed, Elul*, pg. 317)

> *Someone once came to visit Rebbe Noach Lechowitzer and asked for advice which would inspire him with proper humility to begin the teshuvah process. Before Rebbe Noach could respond, the clock began to chime. The Rebbe replied, "That clock is the best motivator, for with every chime an hour of our life has passed."*
>
> (*Otzar Pisgamim Ve'sichos*, pg. 60)

Hashem never rejects a subservient heart. The Maharal explains that a self-effacing person is considered to have offered his own animalistic tendencies to Hashem. Such a sacrifice is always accepted. (*Nesiv Ha'teshuvah* 1)

> *The Baal Shem Tov once instructed his disciple Reb Wolf Kitzis to study the Kabbalistic meditations on which he would meditate while blowing the various blasts of the shofar. Reb Wolf studied the mystical significance of the Divine Names associated with this mitzvah and made notes of them on a sheet of*

paper, which he put away in a pocket so he would be able to read them while blowing the shofar. However, the paper slipped out of his pocket and was lost.

The awesome moment drew near. Reb Wolf searched his pockets in vain, and was obliged to blow the shofar without knowing which Divine mysteries to meditate on. This grieved him to no end, and he wept with a broken and humbled heart.

After the prayers, the Baal Shem Tov said to him: "In a king's palace there are many chambers, and each door has its own particular key. But there is one implement which can open all the doors, and that is the ax.

"The Kabbalistic meditations are the keys to the gates in the World Above, each gate requiring its own particular meditation. But a broken and humble heart can burst open all the gates and all the Heavenly palaces."

On a visit to a certain village Rav Nochum of Chernobyl announced that he would be giving a mussar *lecture on Shabbos afternoon. When he rose to speak he took a good look around. He asked those present if everyone had been informed about the lecture. Everyone nodded. When several latecomers trickled in, those present assumed that the Rav would begin. Time passed and still Rav Nochum waited. Those present started to shift in their seats.*

Humility as an Aid to Teshuvah

Some would have left if not for the fact that Minchah would soon be upon them.

Suddenly Rav Nochum began speaking. Slowly he intoned the mishnah *in* Pirkei Avos *(4:4): "Meod meod hevei shafel ruach, shetikvas enosh rima (Be exceedingly humble in spirit for the anticipated end of mortal man is worms)." He repeated it again and again. Everyone's thoughts were identical: "Is this why he called us together, to repeat a* mishnah *that everyone knows by heart?" If not for their impatience, they would have noticed someone entering the* beis medrash *right before the Rav began. If they had looked carefully, they would have noted the strong impact the words of the* mishnah *had made on him.*

There were two highly respected people in that particular town who excelled in every virtue. They were Torah scholars with good character and fear of Hashem, both of prominent ancestry and blessed with wealth. The son of one married the daughter of the other so that they became related through marriage. The son, too, was blessed with all the outstanding virtues of the father, except that he was haughty. Even when the most respected rabbis came to town to lecture he never attended, believing as he did that no rabbi had anything valuable to offer him. He knew all of Shas and was well versed in all the holy books.

That Shabbos for some reason, he decided to attend Reb Nochum's lecture. Not that he needed any *rebuke, for all his actions were guided by wisdom and fear of Hashem. Yet somehow he felt it essential that he attend. Could it be that he had some deed that needed correction?* he wondered. *He began to review his actions. Could it be that he might have sinned? He highly doubted it. After all, despite his great knowledge, he did not distance himself from the boors. Even though he was wealthy he still learned Torah day and night. He davened with devotion, possessed many good character traits. Why then would he need to attend a* mussar *lecture?*

Yet he found it difficult to stay home. He grabbed his hat and headed out. Still torn between his desire to attend and his feeling that it was beneath his dignity to show his face at the lecture, he wandered aimlessly around town. Before he knew it, he found himself at the door to the shul. When he tried to turn away, his feet appeared to have lost the ability to rotate.

The moment Rav Nochum noticed him, he began repeating the mishnah. *Unlike the others present, the young man felt the words penetrate the wall of haughtiness that had separated him from Hashem and from his fellow Jews. When his emotions ebbed, he hurried to Rav Nochum and begged him to teach him how to repent of this terrible sin.*

(Admorei Chernobyl, pg. 27–28)

The Depths of Heavenly Judgment

The *yetzer hara* goes to great lengths to make us feel detached from the possibility of punishment. He invades our thought processes so we refuse to accept ideas or conclusions that oppose our desires. A person should reflect on the fact that there is nothing worse in the entire world than not paying heed to the commandments of the Exalted King. He must know and believe from the depths of his heart that there is reward and there is punishment, with dire judgments for the transgressions he has committed. Remind yourself that "whoever says that Hashem overlooks sins, will have his life overlooked" (*Bava Kama* 50).

The sinner should not forget that all of the transgressions he has ever committed, both great and small; all of his evil thoughts and idle talk; all of his affairs — small or great — are inscribed in a book. Most people do not realize how penetrating Heavenly judgment is. We must work on heightening our awareness of the consequences of our deeds, remembering the words of *Chazal*: "Contemplate three things and you will not come to sin: know from where you have come, to where you are going, and before Whom you will be making an accounting. Before the King of kings, the Holy One, Blessed is He." (*Avos* 3:1; *Shaarei Ohr* 1:10)

A certain righteous man once hosted the Arizal in his home with great honor. Before resuming his journey the saintly Ari, asked, "How can I repay you for the great affection you have shown me? I would also like to repay you for the trouble you went to on my account."

The host replied that after his wife had given birth to a few sons she mysteriously stopped conceiving. He thought that perhaps the Ari might be able to offer some remedy for her. The Ari responded by first revealing to him the reason for his wife's barrenness. "You know," he said, "that there was once a small ladder in your house upon which the little chicks would ascend and descend to drink water from a nearby loft. In this way they would drink and their thirst would be quenched.

"One day, your wife was cleaning the house and instructed her maid to remove the ladder. Clearly, it was not her intention to cause sorrow to the chicks. But, nevertheless, since the ladder was removed they have been in great distress. Their peeping ascended before Hashem, Whose mercy is on all His works. On this account it was decreed that your wife should become barren."

> *Naturally, the host restored the ladder to its place and Hashem allowed the wife to conceive and give birth as before.*
>
> (Kav Ha'yashar 7)

Although the depth of judgment is hidden from the human eye (*Pesachim* 34b) we have enough clues to get a feeling of what awaits the sinner. We need to summon up the power of our imagination to have an impact on our deeds. When a sinner brought a sacrifice in the days of the *Beis Ha'mikdash*, it was easy to visualize that what was being done to the animal should really have been done to the sinner. Nowadays, we must use the power of our imagination to influence our conscious mind. Contemplation of the harshness of judgment is a useful tool.

Food For Thought

One must remember the whip and the harshness of strict justice … so that you shall be holy to Hashem your G-d" (*Zohar*). Speaking of *Gehinnom*, Rav Yisroel Salanter said, "I am certain of one thing. There they will beat with whips. And it will hurt very, very much. The blows will burn. I am certain of this."

(*Ha'meoros Ha'gedolim*, pg. 185)

> *The Chofetz Chaim tells the story of a young man who turned completely white when about to be shot by*

a firing squad. He writes that we should try to transfer that degree of fear to our own fear of judgment.

The punishment in This World for an unintentional sin, even after teshuvah, is close to two thousandfold (*Chochmah U'mussar I, Maamarim* based on *Kiddushin* 12a). Imagine how those numbers will swell in the World to Come for an intentional sinner. Remember that a person is viewed as an intentional sinner when he repeats the same sin again and again. (*Beitzah* 16a)

The laws of going to war offer another insight into the depths of punishment. A fearful man is sent home. The man is fearful because of the sins he has committed. The *Gemara* explains that this can refer even to one who, in some measure, commits a sin of *rabbinic* origin — unintentionally. He must withdraw from the frontline, lest he die because of this sin. (Rav Eliyahu Mizrachi)

A person should also consider the fact that not only is he punished for every sin no matter how slight, but for each *aspect* of the sin. When Achan helped himself to the booty of Yericho despite the explicit command of Hashem to the contrary, every detail of his crime is enumerated separately (*Yehoshua* 7:21). Each stage of a sin is viewed as a sin in itself: the seeing, the desiring, the taking, and the hiding. When a person does not daven with proper intent he will be punished for each word, each letter each of the Holy Names which he uttered without the proper intent. (Rav Moshe Chaim Luzzato)

In addition, everyone will be rebuked for not making enough of an effort and reprimanded for all they could have done but didn't. We must seek to maximize our potential, striving to use our time and gifts wisely. Rabbi Ezriel Tauber compares the possibilities to various bulb wattages. If a person was born with 200-watt potential and only manages to reach 100-watt potential, he will have to account for this failure. If a person has the potential to make a 75-watt contribution and does so, he is greatly rewarded.

The Chofetz Chaim explains this concept with a parable:

> *A rich man once lent a large sum of money to a poor man so that he could try his hand in business and improve his situation. After a long time, the rich man approached him and asked what he was doing with the money. If the poor man were to reply that he had squandered it on liquor and gambling, the rich man would certainly be very distressed. However, if the poor man has kept it in his wallet the entire time and would now immediately return the entire sum, his benefactor would also be annoyed that he took it for no reason when the rich man could have invested it and increased his profits.*

If a person corrupts his soul with sin, the soul must be weaned away from the corruption. Do we have any idea what pains accompany this process, the repair of a deformation which has become rooted? That process is similar to the pain of a drug addict being weaned off his drug dependence. He screams and roars and wants to jump out of his skin. We call this state of being weaned from deep-rooted corruption *Gehinnom*. Its goal is to remove even the slightest blemish, in order to allow the soul to return in purity.

Exercise

Take a moment to consider the consequences of not being forgiven on *Yom Kippur*.

Teshuvah out of Fear

Reish Lakish said, "If one returns to Hashem out of fear, his sins are converted to involuntary acts. If one returns out of love, his sins are transformed into mitzvos" (*Yoma* 86b). Teshuvah out of fear is teshuvah motivated by fear of punishment both in the Heavenly Court in the World to Come and in This World. It is the body that generally repents, because it is afraid of the punishment that otherwise awaits it. The soul realizes that it can achieve its deep-seated aspiration of clinging to Hashem only through teshuvah and so it is only natural for it to return to Hashem.

Teshuvah out of fear can be compared to not sinning in front of an august personality you want to impress. You will "go the extra mile" in *controlling* your desire, but the negative desire is still there. You have simply repressed it. Therefore this person's wicked deed is not erased totally but is converted to inadvertent sins; still, he will be spared the punishment he fears. (*Kochvei Ohr* 57) To totally erase the damaging residue of the sin one must undertake teshuvah out of love.

> ### INSPIRATION
>
> "For You remember everything that is forgotten" (*Musaf* prayers, *Rosh Ha'shanah*). A chassidic sage once noted: Hashem remembers only those things that a person forgets. If a person has sinned and "remembers," i.e., is conscious of his misdeed and regrets his actions — Hashem "forgets" about the transgression. But if a person sins and is not even bothered by his offense, Hashem does not "forget" so easily.
>
> (*Nahar Shalom*)

"Praiseworthy is the person who is forever fearful, but one who hardens his heart will fall into evil (*Mishlei* 28:14). The fear to which Shlomo Ha'melech refers is a spiritual alertness, a constant vigilance against temptation. Rabbeinu Yonah explains that this is a twofold message to the *baal teshuvah*: "Strive ever higher on the ladder of repentance, and forever be alert to the enticements of the *yetzer hara*, lest it renew itself with added strength as it seeks to undo your spiritual attainments. (Rabbeinu Yonah, *Shaarei Teshuvah* 20).

Rav Moshe Bernstein, son-in-law of Rav Boruch Ber Leibowitz, Rosh Yeshivah of Kamenitz, told the following story: A few years after World War I, I noticed after davening that my father-in-law's facial expression had changed. I asked him what had happened. He told me, shaken and fearful, that he feared he had rendered invalid a certain divorce. That day, among his seforim he had found a sefer with the stamp of the shul of Kremenchov, a city where they had taken refuge during their flight from the approaching army. The sefer had accidentally been mixed among Rav Baruch Ber's possessions and he mistakenly took it along with him as he continued his flight.

Rav Baruch Ber had then passed through Minsk. There the head of the beis din, Rav Eliezer Rabinowitz, invited him to participate in arranging a divorce. Now he feared that the divorce might be invalid, for there is a halachic approach which links the validity of a divorce with the kashrus of the Dayanim who issued it. If Rav Baruch Ber had been in possession of a stolen sefer, perhaps he was not considered a kosher Dayan.

I tried to allay his worries on two counts. One, it was not clear that he was considered a thief, and two, it was not clear that the divorce was truly invalid. But Rav Baruch Ber, with his pure fear of Hashem, could not be calmed. He continued worrying about the matter until he finally remembered that on his way from Kremenchov to Minsk he had been accosted by a band of murderers. He remembered that, just a heartbeat away from death, he recited Vidui and done complete teshuvah for all his past misdeeds. Rav Baruch Ber had then been miraculously saved, continuing on to Minsk. Since he had done teshuvah before arranging the divorce, though he had not been able to return the sefer to Russian territory due to the *danger, he was no longer considered a thief and the divorce was indeed kosher.*

(*Avos Ubanim*)

> ### Inspiration
>
> Every day we have the choice which path to pursue, and that day's decision is wholly independent of the past. One who has made spiritually corrosive, unhealthy decisions throughout life can choose that today's decisions will be growth oriented, spiritually nourishing, and healthful. Likewise, one whose decisions have been spiritually productive cannot rely on past performance to guarantee future results. On any given day, the path of evil is still present as a very enticing option; every day we must make an active decision to avoid sin and live with G-d consciousness.

People tend to greatly underestimate the effects of sin. One who reflects on the greatness of man's duty to his Creator, and on the everlasting evil of the one who disobeys, will never cease to repent, for one can never be sure that his level of teshuvah thus far is sufficient.

The vile creatures created by our sins are restrained by Hashem, awaiting man's repentance. If a person should die without repentance, Hashem releases these destructive entities and they each assault the part of the dead man's body involved in the sin that created them. Surrounding their victim, they carry him off to justice and then send him to the dark and bitter region known as *Gehinnom*. The problem is that most people see this eventuality in the distant future, which is unrealistic, for nobody knows the date of his death. (*Nidchei Yisroel* 28:69–70) All are in agreement that one of the strongest motivating factors to repentance is the knowledge that today might be one's last day.

> One winter morning, two of Rav Saadia Gaon's pupils were walking in the mountains when they heard a strange sound. Approaching the summit, they saw, to their great surprise, their master sitting on the ground, weeping, praying, and engaging in other acts of penitence. What could a tzaddik such as their teacher possibly need to repent for? Could he have committed some sin, G-d forbid? They hurriedly departed, but later that day, they could no longer restrain themselves and asked their teacher the meaning of the scene they had witnessed.
>
> "I do that every day," he said to them. "Every day, I repent and plead with G-d to forgive my shortcomings and failings in my service of Him."
>
> "Your failings?" they asked. "Of what failings does the Gaon speak?"
>
> "Let me tell you a story," said Rav Saadia. "Something that happened to me a while ago.
>
> "One night I was in a small inn run by an old Jew. He was a very kind and simple man, and we spoke for a while before I went to sleep. Early the next morning, after I had prayed *Shacharis*, I bade

him farewell and was again on my way.

"Several hours after I left the inn, some of my pupils arrived there, looking for me. 'Did you see Rabbi Saadia Gaon?' they asked the innkeeper. 'We have reason to believe that he was here.'

"'Rabbi Saadia Gaon?' replied the bewildered old Jew. 'What would the great Rav Saadia be doing here? Rav Saadia Gaon in my inn? No ... I'm sure that you are very mistaken! There was no Rav Saadia Gaon here!'

"But when the young men described me to him, the old Jew grabbed his head and cried: 'Oy! Rav Saadia! Rav Saadia was here! You are right! Oy, Oy!' and he ran outside, jumped into his wagon and chased after me, urging his horse to go as fast as possible.

"Soon, he caught up with me, jumped from his wagon, and fell at my feet, weeping: 'Please forgive me, Rav Saadia! Please forgive me. I didn't know that it was you!'

"I made him stand up and brush himself off, and then said to him: 'But my dear friend, you treated me very well, you were very kind and hospitable. Why are you so sorry? You have nothing to apologize for.'

"'No, no, Rabbi,' he replied. 'If I would have known who you are, I would have served you completely differently!'

"Suddenly I realized that this man was teaching me a very important lesson in the service of Hashem. I thanked and blessed him and returned home.

> "Since then, every evening when I say the prayer before sleeping, I go over in my mind how I served G-d that day. Then I think of that old innkeeper, and say to myself: 'Oy! If I had known about G-d in the beginning of the day what I know now, I would have served Him completely differently!'"
>
> "And that is what I was repenting for this morning."

Rav Saadia Gaon engaged in constant repentance because each day brought him new revelations. If he had known yesterday what he knew today, he would have acted very differently. He was fearful that he had not properly fulfilled his obligation. The same applies to us when we examine our deeds of the recent past. With today's perceptions we would have been more observant yesterday.

Great people take even an inadvertent sin very seriously because they are anxious about the sin it might bring in its wake. Our Sages have taught that sin begets sin (*Avos*). Unless even the minutest sin is eradicated by proper teshuvah, there is no telling what it may lead to.

Teshuvah out of Love

The penitent should be inspired to repent out of love, from a sense of *hakaras ha'tov* (gratitude) to Hashem for the abundant kindness which He has bestowed on him from the moment he entered this world. Hashem has protected him from so much suffering which should have been his lot as a result of his sins. (*Beis Elokim, Shaar Ha'teshuvah* 1:98)

"Since Hashem, in His love, provided him with the ways of repentance, it is fitting that the person should feel indebted to Him and do what He desires." The closer the returnee draws to Hashem the greater his recognition of Hashem's mercy. When we contemplate Hashem's generosity in enabling us to do teshuvah and to totally wipe away our sins no matter how many or how great they are, we recognize the great love that Hashem has for us and His great desire to forgive us and let us continue living. This thought alone should increase our remorse so that we mend our ways. At the same time we are inspired to negotiate ever-greater spiritual heights, and to serve Him with love for the rest of our lives. (*Reishis Chochmah, Teshuvah* 1)

> **Food For Thought**
>
> Although it is impossible to go back in time via a time machine, we can change the past without a time machine — with teshuvah.

Teshuvah out of love of Hashem is the very highest level of teshuvah, in which deliberate sins are transmuted into virtues, when every transgression one has committed is now reckoned to be a mitzvah. With repentance, the distance and disconnection the transgression created have been converted into a force for greater closeness and deeper connection.

This can be compared to the servant who has fled from his master, and who, remembering all the good his master has done for him, returns out of his own volition to implore his forgiveness. (*Orchos Tzaddikim, Teshuvah*)

INSPIRATION

Generally love of Hashem is a prerequisite for any form of repentance. Whereas the person who returns to Hashem out of fear is granted love of Hashem as a gift, one who repents out of love needs no Divine gift.

(*Sefas Emes*)

When this returnee contemplates the "joy" that Hashem derived from his mitzvah and the good it achieved, Hashem gives additional weight to these mitzvos (*Sefas Emes*). Necessarily, this man's sins will be uprooted from their very foundations. Having fulfilled the mitzvah of doing teshuvah, for each of his prior sins he now has an opposite, positive mitzvah: of doing teshuvah. (*Chofetz Chaim II* 1; *Sefas Emes*)

The person who returns out of love is no longer a mixture of good and evil. The person has changed his very essence so drastically that all the facts of his existence, all thoughts, or all action, assume an entirely different meaning and nothing is more important than restoring his relationship with Hashem. He cuts himself off totally from the negativity of the past, and Hashem, in turn does, away with the punishment for this former sinner. When he wishes to give all of his capabilities in the service of Hashem and is ready to suffer a punishment to achieve this closeness to Hashem, he has shifted into another field of being, beyond the cause and effect of our natural world to a supernatural existence.

A Week of Repentance

Between *Rosh Ha'shanah* and *Yom Kippur* we are given a period of seven days, containing every day of the week; one Sunday, one Monday, and so forth. This complete week, neither more nor less, is given to us to enable us to atone and repent for any wrong deeds of the previous year, and to better our way of life in anticipation of the new year. That we have been given a complete week in which to accomplish this is significant: Spending Sunday of this week as we should, and making the most of this time, serves as a repentance and atonement for all the wrong done on all the Sundays of the previous year; the same may be done on the Monday of this week for all the Mondays of the past year, and so on. (*Otzros Rav Eizik Chaver*, pg. 14, in the name of the Ari HaKodesh)

This seven-day period is also a means of planned preparation for the forthcoming year. On the Sunday of this week, we should conside how to better the Sundays of the upcoming new year. This will give us the strength and ability to carry out and fulfill our obligations on the Sundays to come. Likewise, with regard to each of the other days of this week.

> ### INSPIRATION
>
> Why is *Rosh Ha'shanah* before *Yom Kippur*? Wouldn't it be better to first cleanse our sins with *Yom Kippur*, and then face the Judgment of *Rosh Ha'shanah* with a clean slate?
>
> If *Yom Kippur* were first, and we cleansed our sins, then we could very well delude ourselves into believing that we actually deserve a good year due to our virtues. This would be dangerous. We have a better chance if we come to Hashem on *Rosh Ha'shanah* sullied with our sins, and with the realization that we have no merits to rely on. We rely solely on His Mercy. As we conclude the *"Avinu Malkeinu"* prayer: "Our Father, our King, be gracious with us and answer us, though we have no worthy deeds; treat us with charity and kindness, and save us."
>
> (Rav Yisroel Salanter)

A chassid came to the Sefas Emes between Rosh Ha'shanah *and* Yom Kippur *and asked for some business advice. "It is very urgent," he pleaded.*

Answered the Rebbe, "The only urgent thing now is to do teshuvah."

(*Siach Sarfei Kodesh*)

25
Shofar and Repentance

Why do we tremble when the stillness in the shul is suddenly punctured by the piercing pitch of the shofar blasts? What do those sounds mean to us? Why do we find them so deeply moving? The first of the shofar blasts, at the beginning of Elul, signifies the *Shechinah*'s arrival in the camp, and the final blast on *Yom Kippur* signifies the *Shechinah*'s departure. (*Divrei Moed, Elul* 183; *Mateh Ephraim*)

> ### Food For Thought
> The initial letters of the verse "And you shall pass a shofar trumpeting in the seventh month" spell out "teshuvah."
>
> (*Toras Emes*)

The shofar is sounded on *Rosh Ha'shanah* because it is an explicit commandment in the Torah. Nonetheless, it seems to convey a hidden message: "Wake up from your slumber!" it arouses us. "Return to Hashem and remember your Creator! To those who forget the truth and waste most of the year in frivolity and foolishness look into your souls, improve your behavior, and correct your negative ways." (*Hilchos Teshuvah* of the Rambam)

> ### Food For Thought
>
> Can a shofar be blown in a city and the people not tremble? (*Amos* 3:6) Hashem, Who seeks not the destruction of the sinful but their return through teshuvah, calls out to the Jewish people through the blowing of the shofar on *Rosh Ha'shanah* and exhorts them to do teshuvah.

One of the *yetzer hara*'s ambitions is to submerge a person into a routine that deadens his senses. To this purpose, he distracts him with various matters that completely occupy his mind, leaving him no time to contemplate his purpose in the world. But when the shofar is blown in the city and the people do not tremble, their blood is on their own hands. (*Menoras Ha'maor*)

INSPIRATION

The sequence of shofar sounds — *tekiah, teruah, tekiah* — corresponds to three elements of teshuvah. The first

> long sound of *tekiah* symbolizes mans complete break with his sinful ways. The *teruah*'s tremulous wailing sound symbolizes the second stage of teshuvah where the person laments and wails over his transgressions in regret at his sinful days. Finally the *tekiah* is blown again to symbolize the final stage of teshuvah, the deep resolve never to return to the sinful attitudes and deeds.
>
> (Menoras Ha'maor)

If the shofar is a call to repentance, why is the shofar sounded at night, at the close of *Yom Kippur*, when there is as yet no need for a new call to repentance? Clearly, the sound of the shofar also signals an outburst of joyous confidence that our *Yom Kippur* prayers were accepted favorably.

The sounds of the shofar transcend all verbal expression. Human speech is constrained by the limitations of a person's ability to formulate words, to find expressive terminology in his vocabulary, to arrange his words in a form that will accurately reflect and articulate his thoughts. But some thoughts and feelings cannot be articulated or are too exalted to find expression through such limited means. The yearning of the Jewish soul to come close to Hashem, to cleave to the Divine, the wordless groan of an aching heart that longs to return to its spiritual origins, is so intense that mere human speech is inadequate to give it expression. The sound of the shofar, however, connects with this inner yearning and gives it expression. It is the sound of the immortal soul crying out to its Creator in an ecstasy of love, devotion, and aching yearning. It is the sound that breaks the barriers of mere words and embraces myriad spiritual expressions, from the most abject remorse to the most intense joy.

In the same vein, the sounds of the shofar are the expressions of the soul in the purest form. They encompass all sorts of thoughts and emotions that are too amorphous to be clothed in human speech. The call to repentance, the wordless groan, the exuberant joy of *Yom Kippur* night, the mysterious tremble of spiritual longing in the soul of every Jew when he hears the shofar, all these and countless others find expression in the sounds of the shofar.

The shofar conveys the confidential verbal communication devised for use by Hashem and His devoted people. It is like the secret language used by two friends who don't want anyone else to understand their conversation. The accusers of the Jewish nation cannot comprehend the shofar's nuances. (*Tiferes Uziel*)

An analogy is given by the Baal Shem Tov to explain the sounding of the shofar on *Rosh Ha'shanah*:

> *There was once a king who sent his only son to a distant land to learn about its peoples and customs. As time passed, the prince's royal garb became faded and torn, and he even forgot how to speak his native tongue. One day the prince heard that his father, the king, would be visiting the region. "How will I be able to approach him?" he thought.*
>
> *"My clothes are torn, and I cannot speak his language." The son decided that he would simply call out to his father in a cry, without words; a cry emanating from the heart, which the king would surely*

recognize. This is the call of the shofar, it appeals to the King's very Essence.

"From the constraints I call to You and You respond to me from Your most expansive place." We read these and other verses from *Tehillim* seven times, as a way of preparing ourselves for the significant moment of listening to the shofar. The constraint, the place of limitation, is like the mouthpiece of the shofar. That's where we are coming from when we communicate with Hashem. But Hashem, in His great kindness, responds to us in an expansive, open way, likened to the open end of the shofar from whence the sound bursts forth. The words "from the constraints," are at once recognition of where we are and a resolution to go beyond our comfort zone or boundaries.

The shofar is also a wake-up call. The Ohr Gedalya, Rav Gedalya Schorr, *ztz"l*, points out that many of the laws concerning blowing the shofar are derived from the laws of blowing the shofar at the Jubilee Year. Every fiftieth year, all land returned to the family that originally inherited it, and slaves went free. So we see that the call of the shofar is connected to the shofar blast of the Jubilee, which signifies freedom, just as the great shofar at the end of Exile will proclaim our freedom. Here, as well, on *Rosh Ha'shanah*, the shofar is calling for freedom — freedom from the evil inclination.

The shofar cries out: Wake up! You are free! You can set aside all that came before and break the chains — break the patterns of misbehavior and self-destruction which have dogged your path.

> ## Food For Thought
> One must correct the past year by means of repentance. The time of repentance is during the blowing of the shofar.
> (*Igros Kodesh Admor Rav Yosef Yitzchok*, vol. 3, pg. 489)

Rabbi Levi Yitzchok of Berditchev explains why the shofar is such a useful tool in our efforts to achieve atonement by means of a parable.

> *A king was once traveling in the forest and lost his way, until he met a man who recognized that he was the king and escorted his master out of the forest and back to his palace. The king later rewarded him with many presents, and elevated him to a powerful minister's post.*
>
> *After a while, however, the man committed a rebellious act against the king, and he was sentenced to death. Before he was taken out to be executed, the king granted him one last request.*
>
> *The man said: "I would like to be given the chance to slip on the clothes I wore when I saved the king's life in the forest, and that His Majesty should also don the clothes he wore then."*
>
> *The king complied, and when they were both dressed in the garments they wore at the time of their first fateful encounter, the king said, "By*

your life, you have saved yourself," and called off the execution.

When Hashem gave the Torah to the Jews He offered it first to all the nations of the world. They all refused, except the People of Israel, who willingly accepted the yoke of Heaven and fulfilled the commandments of the Creator.

But now we have transgressed and rebelled, like the man in the parable, and with the arrival of the Day of Judgment we are fearful indeed. So we blow the shofar to recall the shofar blowing that accompanied our original acceptance of the Torah and coronation of G-d. This merit stands by us, and G-d forgives us all our sins and inscribes us immediately for a year of goodness and life.

> ### Food For Thought
> *Rosh Ha'shanah* is called the Day of *Teruah* rather than the Day of *Tekiah*, because the middle stage symbolized by *teruah* is the most important. It indicates that one has truly abandoned one's sinful ways and will not readily return to them. Also, the word *"teruah"* is an expression of brokenheartedness.
>
> (*Menoras Ha'maor*)

It is customary to sound a *tekiah gedolah*, a long *tekiah* sound at the end of the shofar blowing, in order to confound the Accuser that he might not bring testimony against the Jewish people for rejoicing with food and drink after their prayers, as if they lacked fear of Divine Judgment. When Satan hears that many more shofar sounds are blown than the Torah prescribes, he is apprehensive, lest he be hearing the shofar of *Moshiach*. In anticipation of Israel's Redemption, he ceases his accusations.

> ### Inspiration
>
> Can it be that the Accuser is so devoid of understanding as to be frightened by the sound of a shofar, which even children know is not the shofar of *Moshiach*? We learn from here that when the Jewish people hear the shofar, they are indeed capable of bringing about their Final Redemption. When they sound their shofros, their impervious hearts are rendered receptive, they shudder over their sins, and in a brief moment their reflections turn to teshuvah. At this point, the sound of the shofar of *Moshiach* can readily be heard. This is what troubles the Accuser. He knows these matters better than we do. He knows Israel's strength and the power of the shofar sounds to bring us to true repentance. The sounds of the shofar may well end with the shofar of *Moshiach* being blown.
>
> (*Sefer Ha'todaah, Tishrei*)

It was the custom of the Shpoler Zeide to closet himself in his study for some time before the blowing of the shofar. What he did there, no one knew. Once, a chassid decided to find out. He crept up to a nook near the Rebbe's private room without being noticed and peered through a crack.

There he saw the Shpoler Zeide lying on the floor, weeping bitterly: "Master of the Universe! What do you want of Your People Israel? If I did not see with my own eyes how many mitzvos and good deeds they perform, I would not believe it possible in this dark and bitter exile to fulfill even one mitzvah! Especially in this benighted world, where Satan himself prances among them, where all things that provoke fleshly desires are before their eyes, while the warnings of retribution You have hidden in some moralistic tome. You can be certain that if You had arranged things the other way around, with the place of retribution in front of their eyes and all fleshly desires hidden away in some learned book, then not a single Jew would ever do anything wrong!"

The Shpoler Zeide then rose from the floor, walked to shul, and proceeded with the blowing of the shofar.

One year Reb Levi Yitzchok of Berditchev spent a long time in search of a man who would be worthy of blowing the shofar in his shul. Rosh Ha'shanah was fast approaching and though many righteous folk sought the privilege, vying with each other in demonstrating their expertise in the abstruse Kabbalistic secrets associated with the shofar, none of them were to his taste.

One day a new applicant came along, and Reb Levi Yitzchok asked him on what mysteries he meditated while he was performing the awesome mitzvah.

"Rebbe," said the newcomer, "I don't understand too much about the hidden things in the Torah. But I have four daughters of marriageable age, and when I blow the shofar, this is what I have in mind: 'Master of the Universe! Right now I am carrying out Your will. I'm doing Your mitzvah and blowing the shofar. So please Hashem do what I want and help me marry off my daughters?'"

"My friend," said Reb Levi Yitzchok, "you will blow the shofar!"

(Rabbi Nissan Mindel, *The Complete Story of Tishrei*)

Rosh Ha'shanah and Yom Kippur were approaching. Reb Levi Yitzchok of Berditchev and Reb Yisroel of Koznitz were preparing for the days ahead. Among the topics they discussed was who would blow the shofar first. They agreed that Reb Yisroel would be given that distinction since he would customarily begin his prayers early.

The morning of Rosh Ha'shanah *had just begun, and the Rebbe of Koznitz ascended the* bimah *to blow the shofar. Concealed by his tallis, he sensed a disturbing, negative response preventing him from blowing the shofar. It was as if the Gates of Heaven were impregnable. Try as he did, he could not breach the wall.*

Suddenly, the gates swung wide open. All the obstacles disappeared and the Heavens were prepared to receive the Jews' prayers.

"What brought about this change?" he inquired. It was revealed to him that the Heavens were penetrated by the holy service of Reb Levi Yitzchok of Berditchev, who was preparing to immerse in the mikveh *before blowing the shofar.*

Reb Yisroel of Koznitz turned to his followers. "If the mere preparations of Reb Levi Yitzchok have such a pronounced effect, we must wait until he blows the shofar, and only afterwards will we proceed with our service."

Reb Yissoschar Dov of Radoshitz took longer than usual on Rosh Ha'shanah *to join the congregants for the blowing of the shofar. When he finally came out of his room, he told his chassidim the following:*

"Let me tell you a story about my Rebbe, the Chozeh of Lublin.

"One Rosh Ha'shanah *the Chozeh remained an extra-long time in his study. He felt unable to leave and join his chassidim for the blowing of the shofar; he was heartbroken at the thought that he had to his*

credit no single merit that would give him the strength to go ahead with this special mitzvah. Finally he remembered that he had, in fact, one merit in his favor: in the course of the previous year he had not spoken one angry word.

"On one occasion, it had almost happened that he lost his temper. His attendant had forgotten to prepare water next to his bed so that he would be able to wash his hands in the prescribed manner in the morning. He had decided to reprimand the attendant for his negligence — until the Chozeh had recalled the warning of the Sages: 'He who is angry, it is as if he worshipped idols.'

"The Chozeh had thought to himself, 'For the sake of the mitzvah of washing my hands in the morning I am going to allow myself, G-d forbid, to become an idolater?' He had therefore said nothing.

"When the Chozeh had reminded himself that he had this one merit to his credit, he went ahead with the blowing of the shofar."

Upon completing the telling of this story, Reb Yissoschar Dov proceeded to lead his own congregation in reading **Tehillim** *47 which speaks of the majesty of the Creator and which serves as the introduction to the blasts of the shofar.*

(*Mipi Chassidim*)

26
Everyone is Urged to Return

No one is permanently pushed away. "The stranger is not forced to pass the night outside" (*Iyov* 31:32). This teaches that Hashem does not disqualify His creatures permanently; rather, He accepts all. "The gates of teshuvah are open at all times; anyone who wishes to enter may do so" (*Shemos Rabbah* 19).

It is necessary to push away the "sinner," to some extent; that is, to let him know that he has gone off the path, but never to reject him entirely. As it says, "A person should always push away the sinner with the left [generally, the weaker] hand, but hold him close with the right [generally, the stronger] hand. Not like Yehoshua ben Perachiah, who pushed away his student with both hands."

According to most opinions, Rabbi Yehoshua ben Perachia was the teacher of Yeshu. Both the *Midrash* and *Gemara* (*Sanhedrin* 107) describes the following fateful series of events that separated the latter from his Jewish origins:

What was the incident involving Yehoshua ben Perachia? When King Yanai killed most of the Sages, two of the small

Because of his talents he was hoping that the Rosh Yeshivah would choose him to marry his daughter. But despite his extensive knowledge, the young man lacked fear of G-d and the Rosh Yeshivah chose someone else. The boy was distraught. In his anger he abandoned Yiddishkeit. He became a journalist for a non-Jewish newspaper. Anti-Semitism was on the rise and he used his column to incite more hatred. Being a former Torah scholar, he cited many quotes from the Torah that appeared to express disloyalty and contempt for non-Jews. He continued his popular column throughout the war years. It is impossible to estimate how much suffering or how many deaths his articles caused. All Romanian Jews knew of him and hated him.

After the war he did teshuvah. He began coming to the beis medrash *of the Skulener Rebbe, then living in Bucharest. The others davening there wanted nothing to do with him. "Traitor!" they shouted. "Get out of here." The man pleaded for their forgiveness but they refused to forgive him. "Who knows how much blood he has on his hands? How can we forget everything and forgive him?"*

The Skulener Rebbe viewed the man in a different light. He welcomed him to his beis medrash *saying, "Hashem accepts all* baalei teshuvah *and we must do the same."*

Was Elisha ben Avuya an exception? We know that a Heavenly voice called out to him that all might return except for him. The Maharsha would have had him ignore that Heavenly voice. (*Chagiga* 15) Hashem was not making it easy for him because of all the grave sins he had committed, but even he would not have been refused if he had made the effort. (*Responsa Maharit II* 8)

Rabbi Yosef MiTrani expands on the *Gemara* that instructs us to do whatever our host asks us unless he tells us to leave (*Pesachim* 86). What the Host of the World tells us to do, we must execute except for leaving His Presence. If teshuvah is what it takes to remain in His presence it is always accessible. Most of the *Rishonim* agree that teshuvah is within reach of even the worst sinner. However, he receives absolutely no help. (*Ohr Ha'teshuvah* 21)

Some people are galvanized into repentance when they are told that repentance is beyond them. Elazar ben Durdiyah (see pg. 251-252) is an example of such a person. On the other hand, when the generation of Yechezkel thought that they could not repent, they gave up. Yechezkel had to tell them that Hashem desires their repentance so that they would turn back to Hashem. (*Yemaleh Pi Tehillasecha*, page 143)

The Greatness of a Baal Teshuvah

The definition of a *baal teshuvah* according to Rabbi Yehudah is: "One who has the opportunity to do the same sin [implying that circumstances are such that his desire to do the sin is the same] and, this time, does not do it! He is a *baal teshuvah*!" (*Yoma* 86b) This is not to suggest that the *baal teshuvah* should *subject* himself to the same temptation for if this were the case, Rabbi Moshe Cordovero would not emphasize that the *baal teshuvah* must return through another route, avoiding his area of weakness. (*Tomer Devorah*; see *Sefer Chassidim* 167)

The Terumas Ha'deshen mentions that someone tried to do teshuvah in the manner Rav Yehudah describes and sinned again. (*Terumas Ha'deshen I*, pg. 136) At all costs he must distance himself from his original sin. The path to purity lies in another direction entirely for it is too difficult to use the original path. (*Shemoneh Perakim* 4; *Asifas Zkeinim, Menachos* 29:2; *Le'hair Le'horos U'le'haskil*, pg. 3–4) If one has fallen into an open well one will be very careful to avoid an unprotected well in the future.

> **Food For Thought**
> Rabbi Abahu said the place where *baalei teshuvah* stand cannot be occupied even by the righteous.
> (*Berachos* 34b)

The true *baal teshuvah* reaches a level of righteousness not matched by someone who has never sinned. Perhaps he never sinned because he was never exposed to temptation. Perhaps by nature he is lazy and apathetic so that the *yetzer hara* has a harder time rousing him to sin. The chamber designated for the *baal teshuvah* is reserved for the person who has remade himself in the image of Hashem. (*Menoras Ha'maor*, Candle 5)

> *Rav Nassan Detzutzisa (Mar Ukva, according to Rashi) was an outstanding* baal teshuvah. *He achieved this status after standing up to great temptation.* (*Rashi*, Sanhedrin *31b*) *When he went out to the market, a candle whose flame rose up to the heavens shone above his head.*
> (*Shabbos* 56b)

This is not as remarkable as it seems for when a person reins in his *yetzer*, taking control of his body like the monarch controls his kingdom, Hashem attaches to him, as it were, a crown like His own — like the candle whose flame rose up to the heavens. This is a living testimony to the fact that he has done complete teshuvah and will never sin again. (Maharal, *Shabbos* 56b; see also *Kochvei Ohr* 87)

The power to return is beyond time. One minute a person is as far as can be, and the next moment he is unified with Hashem. Teshuvah reaches all the way up to the Throne of Glory. One must return out of a powerful desire to do the will of Hashem if one is to achieve the kind of thrust that will lift us all the way to Hashem's Throne. (*Seforno, Devarim* 30)

Moshe Rabbeinu had to climb through the seven heavens — the seven stages of growth and understanding — that the angels taught him before he was entitled to grasp the Throne of Glory (*Zohar, Vayikra* 29b) but the *baal teshuvah* reaches there in one leap. Rav Dessler compares it to a tall building serviced by an old creaky elevator. Healthy people are told to take the stairs, whereas the sick and lame are whisked to the top. Someone who has always served Hashem must toil and strain to climb from level to level until he can complete his part in making known the glory of Heaven but a *baal teshuvah* is carried by Hashem. (*Michtav MeEliyahu*, part 1, pg. 26)

Inspiration

The *Shechinah* envelops a person who is brokenhearted at having been contaminated by sin. Propelled by his distress, the *Shechinah* raises the *baal teshuvah* to the upper spheres, bypassing the tzaddikim who slowly forge upwards. This is because Hashem values a Jew's anguish.

(*Avodas Pnim*)

The longing of the *baal teshuvah* is more intense than that of the tzaddik, the saint who never sinned. His distress over his disconnection from Hashem becomes the things that spur him to greatness. There has been a disruption of the relationship. This fact cannot be undone, but when a person regrets his sins and agonizes over it, his pain translates into a yearning for Hashem more intense than anything the perfectly righteous person can ever experience. As a mirror returns a ray of light that is far more potent than a ray shining directly from its source, so does the *baal teshuvah* return to Hashem with a greater passion and intensity than that of one who never strayed from the straight and true path of connection to G-d through mitzvos.

A person who is far removed from Hashem and decides to return has a vast and difficult expanse to traverse. The greater the distance he must travel back, the more obstacles he has to overcome, the greater is the honor and homage he proffers to Hashem by humbling himself to return to Him. Because he had to work so much harder and travel so much further, his reward is that much greater.

In other words, the further a person has been from Hashem the more honor he displays when he returns to Him. He is often able to exploit his experience and surge higher and higher with greater strength. That is why Hashem cherishes the *baal teshuvah* — because his journey was so much more difficult than that of a righteous person. And that is why one's past sins, which created the distance in the first place and made the return trip so excruciatingly difficult, now become merits, Because every inch traversed on the road back is a declaration of devotion and honor to Hashem.

Having been removed from G-dliness, the *baal teshuvah* wants to make up for lost time, for lost opportunities. His former transgressions, now responsible for his efforts and achievements, are thus sublimated. His descent, in effect, generated his ascent. The former sins are thus converted into actual merits. With his sins reclassified, he automatically rises to a higher level.

The degree of self-sacrifice necessary to undertake a personality overhaul requires strong motivation, because one generally encounters intense resistance. The energy and passion once expended on nonsense and indiscretions are now directed, in ever-increasing measure, towards good. His sinful ardor is converted into positive energy so that he strives upward with all strength, and thus prompted, leaps to levels unattainable by the tzaddik. (*Beer Mayim Chaim, Emor*)

The *baal teshuvah* may experience miracles that are not seen by the righteous because he requires more encouragement due to his handicaps. If Hashem does not reach out to the *baal teshuvah*, he may return to his wickedness (*Sefer Ha'yashar* 10). The *baal teshuvah* may merit that Hashem creates a new universe on his behalf. Whenever the natural order governing this world would deny the *baal teshuvah* any hope of returning to Hashem, Hashem would supersede all natural rules and create a new entity for him. (*Sefas Emes*)

Since the *baal teshuvah* has already tasted sin, he has to exert greater willpower to conquer his desires (than a person who has not sinned). He must muster up more dedication and effort to become a better person than a righteous man in his pursuit of righteousness. He must subdue his heart again and again so that it is re-formed in another, purer mold. (*Sefer Ha'yashar* 10)

> ### INSPIRATION
>
> The very distance that once separated the *baal teshuvah* from Hashem now becomes the vehicle for honoring Hashem. It is as if a person were to travel a thousand miles to catch a glimpse of the king's procession just to stand in the king's proximity for an instant. This is a much more substantial gesture of loyalty than that of someone who lives near the palace who walks a couple of blocks to witness the same procession.

Sin has been compared to a scratch in the king's diamond which the *baal teshuvah* then uses to carve the name of the king. What had previously reduced the stone's value now is responsible for increasing its value. Transgressions impact the spiritual balance of the world; repentance sanctifies Hashem's Name, augmenting the power of Hashem in this world. This is probably what the *Gemara* is referring to when it says, "Whoever offers up his *yetzer* and confesses is viewed by the Torah as having honored Hashem in two worlds: This World and the World to Come" (*Sanhedrin* 43b). Rashi explains that when he repents, slaughtering his *yetzer* and offering it up on the Altar, his sacrifice brings great honor to Hashem.

The Baal Ha'tanya used the metaphor of a rope when he speaks of the relationship between man and Hashem, based on the verse, "Yaakov is the 'rope' of Hashem's portion" (*Devarim* 32:9). When a person sins, he tears this connection asunder, and when he repents, the connection is restored. If we think of the connection as being a rope, then when one does teshuvah the two ends are tied together. When securely knotting a severed rope, it is shortened. This means that the person who does teshuvah now has a closer connection to Hashem than someone who has never sinned, whose rope is at its original length. Similarly the closeness achieved following a quarrel or breach is more intense than the closeness that existed prior to it.

Although it is true that the essence of the tzaddik is always more enviable than that of the *baal teshuvah*, the constant spiritual activity of the penitent results in an immediate closeness in his relationship to Hashem.

> *A wicked Jew approached Rav Moshe De Leon with a smile, asking if it was possible for him to do teshuvah. Rav Moshe replied, "Standard teshuvah would not do for someone such as yourself, who has spent a lifetime sinning. Death is your only atonement."*
>
> *"If I am ready to die, will I receive a portion in the World to Come?" the man asked.*
>
> *"Yes, you definitely will" the Rav replied.*
>
> *The Rav's response penetrated the layers of sin surrounding the soul of the errant Jew. He decided that he was ready to give his remaining allotted years so that he might merit a place in the World to Come.*

Having made that decision, he told the Rav that he was ready to proceed. Together they went to the beis medrash. *The Rav asked that pieces of lead be brought to him in a metal vessel. He lit the fire below the vessel and waited for the lead to melt. The tzaddik then took the penitent, sat him on a chair, and tied a scarf around his eyes. He then told him to confess his sins. Wailing and weeping he began to confess. When he finished, the Rav said, "Repeat after me," and he said the verse of Shema. The crowd that had gathered stood there trembling.*

The Rav then told the man to prepare for death. "Open you mouth so that I can pour in the boiling lead." He called out.

The penitent opened his mouth wide. To the surprise of those present, the Rav reached into his cloak and removed a jar of honey and he proceeded to pour some honey down the throat of the baal teshuvah *as he called out, "May your sins evaporate in atonement."*

When the blindfolded man realized that he had been deceived, he called out, "What have you done, Rebbe? Why have you misled me? Kill me for the honor of the King of kings Who is my Creator. May my body be destroyed so that my soul may live. What is life worth to me when I have sinned so fearfully?"

"Do not worry my son," the Rav reassured him. "Your repentance is complete."

From that day onward, the baal teshuvah did not leave the beis medrash *of Rav Moshe De Leon. He* spent the rest of his life in fasting and repentance, absorbing the teachings of his great Rebbe. Before Rav Moshe passed away, he promised the baal teshuvah that he would try to prepare a place for him near his own in Gan Eden. From the day the tzaddik passed on, the baal teshuvah beseeched Hashem to take his soul, for life without his teacher was not life. After many prayers, the man fell ill and eventually lapsed into unconsciousness. Before his death he opened his eyes calling out, "Make place for Rav Moshe. He has come to keep his promise to me to take me to his side. With that he died. After his death, he appeared in a dream to some of the community elders sitting near his Rebbe."

(Otzar Ha'chochmah)

No Excuses

One of our biggest problems is that we underestimate our potential. We don't realize what we are expected to accomplish and how much we can actually accomplish. We see in front of us a huge mountain to climb and feel that we weren't given the potential to do it. It is certainly true that if Hashem did not help us, we would never be able to overcome our evil inclination. We should therefore ask Him to be our Partner in this important undertaking. (*Mesilas Yesharim*)

How do we know that Hashem will assist us in our efforts to do teshuvah? There is a *Midrash Rabbah* in *Shir Ha'shirim* on the verse: "... the voice of my beloved is knocking; open up ..." (5:2). The *midrash* cites Rav Yasa, who says, "Hashem says to the Jewish people, 'Open up for me an opening of repentance [even as little as] the size of an eye of the needle, and I will open for you openings [so big] that even wagons will be able to pass through.'" We just have to make the initial move towards repentance, and then Hashem will help us go further.

The Alter of Novardok asks, "Haven't we opened up an opening at least of a needle? So why hasn't Hashem responded with a big opening?" He answers that there are different materials in which holes can be made. If you make it in sand, it doesn't last. But, if you make it in metal it will last. That's why the *midrash* stresses "the size of an eye of the needle," to indicate that the opening has to be an enduring and constant commitment, not just a temporary spark of repentance. Our temporary openings will never result in the desired effect.

> ### INSPIRATION
>
> "Open up just an opening the size of an eye of the needle in teshuvah for Me — as long as it passes through and through" (Kotzker Rebbe). That is to say that man is not permitted to be satisfied with a small teshuvah, even though he is capable of achieving much more. In reward for returning to Hashem in teshuvah, in full accordance with his knowledge and ability, a man's eyes are illuminated and "huge doorways" open before him. Such a man will realize that his first teshuvah was only a mere, inadequate pinprick.
>
> (*Emes Me'kotzk Titzmach*, section on Teshuvah, 158 and 172)

The *mishnah* in *Avos*: "If I do not do for myself, who will do it for me? And if I do only for myself what am I?" (1:14) teaches us that if a person doesn't start by working on himself, then even Hashem will not help him. But when I begin working on self-improvement, I will not succeed unless Hashem helps me. (See *Mesilas Yesharim*, end of ch. 2.)

Because man alone cannot effect a complete atonement, Hashem gathers up the penitent and implants within him a new heart and a new spirit (*Yechezkel* 36:26). Hashem assists the person who demonstrates his desire to come close to Him in repentance. As it says, "Hashem is good and just; therefore, he guides sinners in the path" (*Tehillim* 25:8).

From the moment a person decides to keep the Torah, his inner spark is ignited and it draws him towards Hashem.

Food For Thought

Man need only sincerely wish to repent. Without even having done anything about it, already then Hashem reaches out and helps him to achieve his wish. The mere decision to return to Hashem, even though he has not actually begun, gives life to the soul. Hashem awaits these initial steps. Having done the best we can do, though it is no more than a minute effort, we will ultimately reach awesome heights that are totally out of proportion to our actions. We must only do what we can, on our part. (*Beis Elokim, Shaar Ha'teshuvah* 1) and then Hashem will guide us along the path to complete return, helping us attain even that which is not within man's power, so that all components of teshuvah are fulfilled.

(*Orchos Tzaddikim, Teshuvah*)

Because the *baal teshuvah* is not schooled in fighting his *yetzer hara*, Hashem assists him in his resistance. (*Maor Ve'shemesh*)

In *Tanna De'bei Eliyahu Zuta (14), Eliyahu Ha'navi* relates: "Once I was going from place to place and I met an ignorant man who knew neither Chumash nor Mishnah and he was scoffing at me. I said to him, 'My son, what will you answer your Father in Heaven on the Day of Judgment?'

"He replied, 'Rebbi, I have what to answer Him. They didn't give me from Heaven understanding and knowledge to learn Chumash and Mishnah.'

"I then asked him, 'What is your profession?'

"He replied, 'A fisherman.'

"I countered, 'And who taught you to bring flax and weave it into nets, throw it into the sea, and catch the fish?'

"He answered, 'Rebbi, for this they gave me understanding and knowledge from Heaven.'

"Finally I said [in wonderment], 'For bringing flax to make nets to throw into the sea to catch fish — for this they gave you understanding and knowledge from Heaven — and for words of Torah, about which it is said [Devarim 30:14]: "For it is very close to you this concept [Torah] in your mouth and in your heart to do it." For that they didn't give you understanding and knowledge from Heaven?'

"At that point the fisherman [who realized how foolish he looked with his erroneous logic], began to cry. I told him, 'My son, don't feel bad, because all the other people in the world give this excuse [about not being given understanding and knowledge for Torah]. And yet their own deeds [the understanding and knowledge of their own profession] refute this excuse.'"

There was a prince who lived a long way from his father. "Return to your father," his friends told him. "I can't," he replied. His father sent him a message, "Go as far as you can, and I will meet you the rest of the way." Thus Hashem says to the Jewish people. "Return to me, and I will return to you." (*Zecharyah* 1:3; *Pesikta Rabbasi* 45:9)

"The evil inclination attacks us daily. If Hashem did not help us we would not withstand it" (*Succah* 52b). Our only hope is to cry out to Hashem constantly, "Open the gate for me" (*Yalkut Shoshanah*).

29

Hashem Helps

But we must know that there is no such answer as "I can't." As long as we do what we are obligated to do, Hashem will help us. "The Torah explains that Hashem will help those who repent when it is not in their nature to do so. He will renew in them a spirit of purity to reach the level of loving Him." (Rabbeinu Yonah) In other words, even if according to natural laws he really can't repent, because "it is not in his nature to do so," Hashem creates special circumstances, triggering a spirit of purity until he reaches the level of His love.

"A poor man, a rich man, and a wicked man come to [final] Judgment. To the poor man they say, 'Why did you not learn Torah? ....Were you poorer than Hillel.... [And yet he managed to learn]?' To the rich man they say, 'Why did you not learn Torah?' If he says he was too busy with his property, they respond, 'Were you richer than Rabbi Elazar ben Charsom [who despite his wealth managed to learn]?' To the wicked man they say, 'Why did you not learn Torah?' If he says he was handsome and preoccupied with his *yetzer hara*, they respond, 'Were you more handsome than Yosef [who withstood the attempted seduction by Potiphar's wife (*Bereishis* 39:7)]? [So too you should have conquered your *yetzer hara*].'" (*Yoma* 35b)

According to one view, Yosef was actually ready to give in to Photiphar's wife, but he was saved by a miraculous vision of his father (Rashi, *Bereishis* 39:11 and *Gemara Sotah* 36b). How can the wicked be held accountable, if Yosef was saved only through the miracle of the vision and not as a result of his own strength, and the wicked do not merit such miracles?

Had Yosef's salvation been through his own natural strength, Yosef would be held accountable. But since his salvation came through miraculous, Divine help how can the wicked be held accountable?

Yosef merited miraculous Divine help because he withstood all the seductions and punishments that the wife of Potiphar threatened him with. He fought his *yetzer hara* with all of his might until he could go no further. Only then did Hashem intervene in the form of a vision. (*Tuvcho Yabiu*, vol. II, pg. 286, in the name of Rav Yisroel Salanter)

Anyone who uses his potential to its fullest to conquer his *yetzer hara* and can't go further will also receive miraculous Divine help. Based on the *gemara* in *Kiddushin*, it's logical to deduce that Hillel and Rabbi Elazar ben Charsom also had tests beyond their strength and only because they used their potential to its fullest did they merit Divine intervention. Therefore, in light of the deeds of these giants, all of us are accountable, despite the fact that our natural strengths don't come anywhere near theirs.

Rabbi Chaim Shmulevitz, points out that every time we do what is commanded of us, it is Hashem who brings the results. It is incumbent on a person only to act, not to accomplish. Any other approach is a declaration of "my power and the might of my hand have gotten me all this success" (*Devarim* 8:17). While this injunction literally applies to physical endeavors and accomplishments, it applies to the spiritual as well.

This idea finds expression in the prayer of Rabbi Nechunya ben HaKanah (*Berachos* 28b): "I toil and am rewarded. For it is for the effort itself that man is rewarded, not for the result. The accomplishment and attainment is a part of the *reward*."

With this point he answers an apparent contradiction. It says in *Pirkei Avos* (4:1): "Who is strong? He who subdues his evil inclination." On the other hand, it says in *Gemara Succah* (52b), "Were it not for the assistance of the Holy One, [man] could not conquer [his evil inclination]." How then can Chazal attribute the subordination of the evil inclination to strength?

Rav Chaim responds: "The answer is that Hashem's help is commensurate with a person's efforts. Man battles; Hashem conquers. If a person has succeeded in overcoming his evil inclination, it is indeed testimony to his strength." (*Reb Chaim's Discourses*)

Inspiration

Teshuvah involves two types of rectification. The first involves breaching the wall erected by our evil deed. The second involves rectifying the damage wreaked on the cosmos due to our deeds. The first is rectified by our deeds. The second is rectified by Hashem. This is the way the Brisker Rav explains the verse, "For on this day he shall provide atonement for you to cleanse you from all your sins. Before Hashem shall you be purified" (*Vayikra* 16:30). The word "atonement" is a reference to the first rectification, executed by man. The purification of the cosmos, however, must be done by Hashem.

(Al Ha'teshuvah, pg. 15)

Two Types of Purification

Rabbi Akiva describes how fortunate we are, the Jewish people, for it is Hashem alone, our Father in Heaven, who purifies us when we sin. The *Mishnah* cites two verses supporting this premise, one from *Yechezkel* (36:25): "And I [Hashem] will sprinkle pure water on you, that you may be purified."

Then the *Mishnah* cites another verse from *Yirmiyahu* (17:13): "The Mikveh of Israel is Hashem." Rabbi Akiva explains: "Just as a *mikveh* purifies those who have become defiled, so too Hashem purifies the Jewish nation." (*Yoma* 85b)

Rav Avraham Yaakov Pam points out that the *Mishnah* mentions two distinct types of purification. The first is immersing in a *mikveh*. The second type is "sprinkling," which refers to the sprinkling of the water on the ashes of the *Parah Aduma* (Red Heifer) in *Parshas Chukas* 19.

Rav Hirsch, the son of Rav Yitzchok Elchanan Spector, explains why both types of purification are mentioned. He points out a major halachic difference between the two types.

A *mikveh* will purify only one who is completely immersed in the water, without even one hair sticking out. On the other hand, regarding the water of the Red Heifer, we are told that even if it only fell on one limb — even on the tip of his finger or on his lip — it purifies the person.

The process of teshuvah encompasses both concepts. There is the repentant sinner who returns with all of his heart and becomes a totally different person. This is like the complete immersion in the *mikveh*. Then there is one who returns only slightly and rectifies only a few of his sins. This is like the sprinkling of a little water on the tip of his finger.

This is why the *Mishnah* mentions both types of purification. It teaches that if a person cannot reach the higher level of complete purification, then he need not give up. He should at least try to reach the lesser level, of "sprinkling on the tip of the finger." And even though the sprinkling is not enough and he still needs complete purification, at least this is a beginning.

These two types of purification may refer to two types of repentant Jews. There are those who repent of their own volition. They come on their own, so to speak, to the *mikveh* to be purified. To them the first verse applies, that talks about the *mikveh*. Rav Yaakov Galinsky compares it to two patients who share a room in the hospital. Both are very sick and need medicine to survive. The future looked bleak for both of them. However, there is one major difference between them. The first patient can at least reach out for his pills lying on the tray in front of him. The second patient is so weak that he can't even get his own medicine. He is totally dependant on others. If no one comes, his end will surely come.

The very ill are those who have, unfortunately, strayed so far from the true path of Judaism that it seems almost futile to hope that they will return on their own. Or maybe they have only a veneer of religious commitment, covering a very distant soul. In those instances, though, Hashem doesn't wait for the person to come to the *mikveh* to be purified. Rather, Hashem "goes out" to the person, and "sprinkles pure water" on the defiled Jew, so that he may be purified and return to the fold.

Rabbi Yaakov Galinsky points out: "How fortunate indeed are the Jewish people, that Hashem does not forsake them. Even when some of them are rebelling against Him and not looking to be purified, Hashem, in His mercy, sprinkles water on them [with an unexpected occurrence that awakens them from their spiritual slumber] so that they may return to Him."

Hashem's "sprinkling" comes in many forms. Hashem may even send a heat wave to start a person on the road to repentance.

Rav Nota Weiss, a maggid *in Yerushalayim, would address the public every Shabbos. One week there was a heat wave. The temperature was so unbearable that the streets were deserted. However, Rav Nota was determined to fulfill his obligation despite the sweltering heat. He said to himself, "Even if no one shows up I am obligated to give my lecture."*

When he arrived in the empty shul he walked up to the aron kodesh, *put on his tallis, and began his usual fiery talk. He spoke for two hours as he did every Shabbos. When he finished, a young man emerged from the women's section, fell to the Rav's feet, and cried out, "Rebbe! I am ready to repent."*

Rav Nota later found out that the young man had wandered into the shul to escape the heat and lain down in the women's section, where he fell asleep. Rav Nota's voice roused him, and he sat back to listen to the lecture.

True to his word, he became an earnest penitent.
(Sheaal Avicha Ve'yagedcha, page 142)

Sprinkling can take the form of "chance" meetings or notes falling from the Kosel.

Meshulam waited until the last possible moment to tell his father that he was leaving for India. His stunned father jumped into the departing taxi in a last-ditch attempt to talk his son out of self-destruction. All the way to the airport the father begged the errant boy to reconsider. He implored him not to abandon all that was precious and dear to a Jew. Meshulam's heart remained closed to his father's pleas. He was determined. In despair, his father called after him as he walked towards the gate: "I don't want to see you ever again. I will never forgive you."

Those were the last words Meshulam heard from his father. In India he put aside the trappings of his Yiddishkeit and sank into the depths of impurity. From time to time he remembered his father's intense grief. He even made some attempts now and then to phone his father but there was no answer. He tried writing him but received no reply. One day he bumped into an old friend. His friend was shocked at his decadent appearance. His discomfort was apparent and he said, "I'm really sorry to have heard about your father."

"About my father? What happened to him"? Meshulam asked.

His friend looked at him in disbelief. "Your father died months after you left, of a heart attack. They said the heart attack was caused by his great anguish at your abandonment of Judaism. Didn't you know?"

Meshulam fell into a deep depression. His heart was filled with grief and he lost the will to live. His friends couldn't cheer him up. Finally, one day, he climbed out of bed and announced that he was going to Israel. His friends made fun of his suggestion but he bought a ticket on the first possible flight.

As soon as he arrived he took a taxi straight to the Kosel. He lay his head on the worn stones and cried, for the past and for the present and for the dark and gloomy future. He cried out for the terrible grief he had caused his father. How could he ever attain forgiveness for such a great sin? The hot tears welling up from the innermost chambers of his heart ran down his cheeks, forming a small puddle at his feet.

"Father, Father," he cried out from the depths of his heart. "Forgive me for all the sorrow and anguish

I have caused you. I never meant to hurt you. Please daven on my behalf to our Father in Heaven. For me to carry on, you must give me a sign that you can hear me!" he implored.

An elderly man, who had been standing next to him and heard his cries, advised him to write his request on a piece of paper and insert it in the Wall. Taking a pen in hand, he painfully sought to condense his heart's appeal for forgiveness onto a piece of paper.

He then looked for a crack in which to place his slip of paper, addressed to his father upon whom he had brought such intense suffering. But every time he put the note into the Wall, it slipped out and fell to the ground. He feared that he was receiving a Heavenly message that his sins were too terrible to be forgiven. Finally he tried to find a place higher up, in one of the deeper cracks of the wall. This time, the paper remained in place and didn't fall out, but from that very same crack, crammed with many such notes, another paper fell to the ground. As he picked it up, he noticed his own name written on the outside in what looked like his father's handwriting.

He opened it and began reading its contents: "Almighty G-d, please have mercy and pity on my son Meshulam son of Rivkah, who has traveled to India. I love and treasure him and I fully forgive him from the very bottom of my heart for all he has done to me. When I parted from him at the airport, I got very angry and said that I would never forgive *him. But I've since had a change of heart, and now truly forgive him for everything he's done to me. I pray to You, our Father in Heaven, that You too forgive him and that You put the will into his heart and mind to repent for his sins. I pray that the day will soon come that he will marry a true, religious, G-d-fearing girl and merit to raise holy, pure children who will live a life of Torah and mitzvos."*

When Meshulam finished reading the letter, he sat down and began to sob like a baby. By the time he left the Kosel, he was a full-fledged baal teshuvah.
(*Aleinu Le'shabeiach, Devarim II, Nitzavim*)

The Akeidas Yitzchok describes four types of repentant Jews in a comparison of a man lost in the woods who cannot find his way back to the city. Some people will immediately orient themselves using a compass and find the road that will lead them home. These are the people who are alert to any sin and repent immediately. As it says, "That the deeds of man [may follow] the word of Your lips, I have preserved [my soul] by avoiding the way of the lawbreakers" (*Tehillim* 17:4). Such a person is constantly on the alert to avoid the way of the lawbreakers.

The second person's sense of direction is not so sharp. Scanning the horizon, he notes roads weaving up a hill in the distance and he walks in that general direction while keeping his eyes on the mountain. This is like one who consults with the *seforim* of the ancients to learn the right path he must pursue.

The third person is not discerning enough to notice the

mountain trail. He wanders about looking for some farmer or shepherd who can tell him how to get back to the city. This is like one who seeks out a Rav who can regularly advise him in the art of self-improvement.

Finally, there are those who are lost and incapable of finding a way out. The best that can happen to them is that someone will discover them before they fall prey to the wild animals and robbers that frequent the forest. Unfortunately, there are those who are not discovered by anyone, but when they fall and injure themselves in the underbrush, or an animal attacks them, desperation empowers them. At that point they do not stop searching until they find a way out. Sometimes only suffering, *Rachmana litzlan*, induces the person to return to the solid path of Torah. (*Akeidas Yitzchok* 100)

The Significance of Elul

We can attain great heights in teshuvah, Torah, and service of Hashem during Elul, with comparatively little effort, compared with the rest of the year. Because during this time, following the sin of the Golden Calf, while Moshe Rabbeinu was up in Heaven, the Jewish people were fasting and doing teshuvah, setting the standards for future generations. (*Tanna De'bei Eliyahu Zuta*; *Chayei Adam* 138:1)

That unique environment of repentance and forgiveness is accessible to us year after year during this time. If we are spiritually sensitive, the strains of repentance will penetrate our heart and stir our soul to contrition. (See *Birchas Avrohom*, pg. 121.) It is important to capitalize on this month since if we let this chance go by, not only do we lose a golden opportunity, but it is also tantamount to showing that we are not interested in doing teshuvah, *Rachmana litzlan*. Ideally, having repented in Elul, we will be among those for whom Tishrei will truly be a "*Mikra Kodesh*," a holy convocation with the *Shechinah* resting upon us (*Arvei Nachal, Emor, Derush* 2).

On *Rosh Ha'shanah* we are reborn (*Vayikra Rabbah* 30:3). As it says in *Tehillim* (22:32): "They will come and declare His righteousness to a newborn people." This would make Elul the last month of gestation. When a woman is expecting a baby she relishes any moving sensation, for it is an indication that the baby in her womb is alive and kicking. When there is no movement, she is fearful that something might be wrong with the child. If Elul is the equivalent of the last month prior to birth, then movement and growth are synonymous with good tidings (*Netziv Derashos, Derush III* and *Derush IV*).

Inspiration

"She shall ... sit in your house and weep for her father and mother for a full month" (*Devarim* 21:13). The Ohr Ha'chaim explains that every sinning soul should find a special place to call its own and tearfully confess for having rebelled against her father, Who is Hashem, and her mother, who is the Jewish people, for a month. This hints at the month designated for teshuvah — Elul. The *sefer Likutim of the Arizal* (*parshas Ki Seitzeh*) adds that during this time the captive woman should "shave her head," getting rid of negative thoughts; "let her nails grow," as she divests herself of any stolen item; and "remove her garment of captivity," the garment of sins she has crafted.

(*Parshas Ki Seitzei*)

"From the onset of Elul until the close of *Yom Kippur* one should feel awe and dread of the upcoming judgment" (Rabbeinu Yonah). In previous generations, the fear of Hashem was sound, but their evil inclination swayed them to sin. When Elul arrived, their fear of Hashem prevailed and they were overcome with fear and remorse.

Although with each passing generation the arousal ought to be stronger and stronger due to increased sinfulness, in reality it has become weaker and weaker. Speaking of this phenomenon, Rav Yisroel Salanter writes, "It is not as one might think, that the man who all year was distant from Hashem's service now became wrapped in dread and fear of the impending judgment.... Rather, it was the very opposite. A change for the better was seen much more in the man who all year long treaded a path of holiness according to his worth than it was in the man who, according to his own worth, walked all year in darkness, with nary a ray of light."

The reasons for this difference are both natural and spiritual. It is natural for man's behavior to be dictated by habit, whether for good or for bad. The spiritual reason is likewise simple enough, for when man sins, he draws upon himself a spirit of impurity which sullies his spirit and confuses his thinking. In the words of our Sages, "A man does not sin unless a spirit of folly enters into him" (*Sotah* 3a). Unfortunately this spirit does not fear the Day of Judgment.

Nowadays, because people are so distant from Hashem, they do not feel the effects of Elul. According to Reb Itzele Peterberger, our more sinful generations should begin their teshuvah on *Rosh Chodesh Shevat* to give ourselves enough time to finish by *Yom Kippur*.

Certainly, as intelligent people, we must rouse ourselves to repentance in the beginning of Elul, preparing ourselves for the great judgment of *Rosh Ha'shanah*, in which our fate will be decided. Repentance and prayer should be at the forefront of our endeavors during this month. (Meiri, *Ha'teshuvah* 2:1) Remember that all the suffering of the upcoming year is, *Rachmana litzlan*, decreed on *Rosh Ha'shanah*. Our lives hang by a thread. Is it possible that there is anyone who is not fearful? The Alter of Kelm or, alternately, Rav Yitzchok Zev Soloveitchik, offers a parable for variable attitudes towards Elul preparation.

> *A poor merchant learned that it was possible to sell his merchandise on the other side of the border for a much higher price. He sought a professional smuggler knowledgeable of the byways near the border, capable of staying on track during the pitch-black cover of night, familiar with the border guard patrols' comings and goings, and last but not least, with nerves of steel for such a risky enterprise. When he found someone who fit the bill, they chose a site for the crossing at a point where the guards were likely to be less alert and fixed a date for a moonless night.*
>
> *A month before the scheduled rendezvous, the Jew was suddenly beset by fear. He knew that, if caught, he risked his livelihood, possessions, and even his life. On the other hand, the wagon driver, who made much of his livelihood through this type of clandestine pursuit, still had his wits about him*

and remained calm. A few days before the appointed time, the smuggler also began to fear for his life, and wondered whether he ought to consider another profession. There was one partner in this criminal venture that remained calm from beginning to end, and this was the team of horses that drew the wagon.
(Divrei Moed Elul)

The lesson is readily understood. Like the merchant, some take the approaching "days of awe" quite seriously and with the advent of Elul they begin their soul-searching, contemplating the crossing of the border — i.e., the passing before Hashem. Others are like the wagon driver, and only "get to work" from the time we begin saying *selichos* prayers, or on the eve of *Rosh Ha'shanah* itself. Last, and least, unfortunately there are those who are like the team of horses, who feel absolutely nothing. Their *Rosh Ha'shanah* and *Yom Kippur*, come and go and their life goes on with no impact and no resolutions.

Rav Yechezkel Levenstein once explained that in Europe one was expected to sweep clean the dirt or shovel the snow from in front of his house. Anyone failing to do so would be fined and could even receive a hard blow from a policeman's stick. Even at the last moment, just before the policeman would turn the corner, one could grab the shovel and get to work! In Elul as well, Hashem awaits our teshuvah — even in the waning moments of the month. The *Mashgiach* would exhort his students to "grab onto the shovel — do teshuvah — and return to Hashem." He would emphasize that once a person begins to turn away from sin he is already in a state of teshuvah, and his status before Hashem is completely different. He is working — shoveling! And even if he does not complete the job, even if his teshuvah is incomplete, he should keep going. (*Reb Chatzkel*, pg. 193

> ### Food For Thought
>
> In the days prior to *Yom Kippur*, we ought to picture a man with a rope tied around his neck, standing on a chair with someone standing at his side ready to kick the chair away.
>
> (Alter of Novardok)

A person may remain tranquil and serene while acknowledging some sins because he feels confident that he has bundles of mitzvos to offset them. This, of course, is merely a ploy of the *yetzer* to keep him from doing teshuvah. To counteract this overconfidence, we should consider the *midrash*: "Woe is to us from the Day of Judgment, woe to us on the Day of Reproof" (*Midrash Rabbah, Vayigash* 93). Bilaam, the prophet and leader of the nations, could not endure the criticism of his donkey. Yosef was the youngest of the tribes, yet his brothers could not face his rebuke. Remember that although we may now think we have ready answers, we will likely be in the same position as Yosef's brothers whose rationalization for their behavior immediately dissolved when Yosef revealed that he was the brother they had sold.

> *In the frightening days of tyrannical police power in the former Soviet Union, any practicing Jew walking the streets of Moscow lived with a lurking fear of being picked up by the dreaded KGB on trumped-up charges that could land him in an all-expenses-paid vacation to picturesque Siberia. Imagine a Jew walking down the street when suddenly an unmarked police vehicle pulls up and two men jump out and "help" him into the car. The driver says, "You are being taken to headquarters to be tried for some major crimes." Having no choice, our hapless comrade enters. Thoughts of never seeing his family again, of endless fields of pristine ice accompanied by a mean temperature of 40 degrees below zero in the Gulag Archipelago, even of a firing squad, pass before his eyes.*
>
> *Suddenly the vehicle comes to a stop in a dark desolate narrow roadway. The driver exits and asks his passenger to do likewise. He then says to the passenger, "I know that you are Jewish. I too am Jewish. The tribunal I am bringing you to is the Heavenly Tribunal. Rosh Ha'shanah is almost upon us and you, as well as everyone else, are being brought in front of the Heavenly Court to be judged for life or for ..." The hapless passenger breathes a great sigh of relief. "It is only in front of Hashem that I am*

being brought! That is the best news I've heard in a long time. I thought that I would be sitting in front of the Communist judges!"

(*Lekach Tov*)

Just think of the worst-case scenario in a Russian court on this short-lived world and compare this with the Judgment of Hashem, and rulings that last forever and forever. Use the power of your imagination to try to evoke a dramatic sense of urgency within you.

A feeling of awe enveloped the large shul as the sons of the Tzemach Tzedek took their places around the bimah, *each in his designated place. The Tzemach Tzedek himself finished his preparations, readying himself to blow the* tekiyos. *His face burned brightly as he sang softly to himself, his eyes closed in deep concentration. Suddenly his voice resonated throughout the shul, "Woe! My heart! A Psalm ..."*

Panic gripped the congregation and tears flowed freely. Some evil decree prompted the Rebbe's unusual outburst, no doubt, and a great wailing filled the shul. Everyone's heart was open, raw and receptive. The congregation recited the psalm seven times as required and the Rebbe began the shofar blasts....

Hopefully many people have an appreciation of the fact that Elul is such an important time that they must certainly try to utilize it. Such a person has already chosen which *mussar sefer* to learn, which *shiurim* he will attend, and which *middos* he will work on. But even here the *yetzer* goes to work, making the person feel overconfident to the point where during the entire month he basks in his lofty goals, but never takes a penetrating look at his real self. Without this, true teshuvah is unlikely.

Our emotions in the beginning of Elul should reflect the sentiments of a village that has just been informed that their benevolent monarch is coming to visit in a month. Their first reaction may be concern: petty crime is rampant and the town is quite run down with alleyways full of garbage and paint peeling on many public buildings. Certainly there will be people disciplined for that neglect, but still the underlying feeling is joy at the king's visit. The people love him and he loves them and they look forward to seeing him.

Asking Others for Forgiveness

The Ten Days of Repentance should be spent in thoughts of teshuvah to prepare for the purification which will come on the final day of *Yom Kippur*. While on *Rosh Ha'shanah* we are judged by Hashem's Heavenly Court; on *Yom Kippur*, Hashem judges us. Therefore everyone must cleanse himself of sins against Hashem and sins against his fellow man.

Repentance and the Day of Atonement atone only for sins committed against Hashem, such as eating a forbidden food, having prohibited relations, etc. To gain atonement for sins against other human beings, such as injuring, cursing, stealing, etc., we must first gain the forgiveness of the person we sinned against, making good any monetary damages or debts. Even after paying any money due, we must still discuss the sin with the person we sinned against and ask for forgiveness. This is especially vital before *Yom Kippur*, for there is no other way to gain Hashem's forgiveness for our interpersonal sins. (*Orach Chaim* 606:1)

The only way to proceed is to recall all the people we have hurt and ask for their forgiveness. We must try again and again, expressing our pleas for forgiveness in different ways, even bringing along others who may convince the offended party that we earnestly seek his forgiveness. (*Chayei Adam* 154–155)

> *It is said that Rav Akiva Eiger never became angry at anyone — never that is, except once.*
>
> *He was then the head of a large yeshivah in Lisa. He learned that one of his students was not behaving as a yeshivah student should. Rav Akiva summoned the boy to his home and when it became evident that the information was correct, Rav Akiva became very angry and ordered the student to leave the yeshivah immediately. Fifteen years passed. Rav Akiva had left Lisa and was now Rav of Friedland. One day, he learned that the young man was living in Breslau. As soon as he heard that, Rav Akiva wrote him a letter.*
>
> *"Fifteen years ago," he wrote, "when you were a student of mine in Lisa, I lost my temper and shouted at you. I have never forgiven myself, and my words have caused me deep pain and sorrow. All these years, I did not know how to make amends, for I didn't know where you lived. Now that I obtained your address, I sat down immediately to write you a letter of apology. Please forgive me for having gotten angry at you. Relieve my troubled soul and let me know that you do not bear be any ill will."*
>
> (*Ha'machaneh Ha'chareidi* #1331)

Asking Others for Forgiveness

Every night, after reciting the last blessing of the bedtime prayers, the tzaddik Reb Yitzchok of Drohovitz lay his head on his pillow, closed his eyes, and fell fast asleep. One night his soul refused to ascend to the celestial realms. He tossed and turned in his bed, sleep refusing to come to him. He couldn't understand why.

Reb Yitzchok sat up in his bed and began pondering his day, minute by minute, word by word, and thought by thought. And then, it came to him in a flash! Of course, that was it!

That afternoon, he had overheard a conversation in which the Baal Shem Tov had been maligned by a certain Jew. Reb Yitzchok was about to reprimand the speaker, but then, for some reason now unclear to him, he refrained and was silent.

Reb Yitzchok knew what he must do. He quickly jumped from his bed and put on his clothes. He saddled his horse and rode through the night, never stopping until he dismounted in Mezibuzh, right in front of the Baal Shem Tov's shul.

When Reb Yitzchok entered the shul, he saw they were in the middle of Shacharis. *He stood there for a few minutes, contemplating the scene, when a strange thing happened — someone called his name. He was being honored by being called up to the Torah. "That's strange," he thought as he stepped forward to the* bimah, *"no one knows me here. I wonder how it is that I am being called."*

When Shacharis *was over, Reb Yitzchok had no*

chance to beg forgiveness. The Baal Shem Tov strode up to him, hand extended, and said quite simply, "Yisroel forgives you from the bottom of his heart."

(Mipi Chassidim)

The Maggid of Kelm never traveled after noon on Erev Shabbos. One Friday found him still far from his destination. He ordered his driver to stop at the nearest Jewish village. When he arrived, he asked the first Jew he met whether there were any spiritual failings in the community he might address as a speaker. The man shook his head. "This is a solid, G-d-fearing community with numerous study groups and a plethora of charitable activities," he replied.

The Maggid persisted. "We are taught that there is no righteous person who has never sinned. Surely, there must be something that needs correction." The man furrowed his brow in thought. "Yes," he finally replied, "there is one problem the city suffers from and that is Yankele the Mossur. He is a degenerate miscreant who maligns the Jews, consistently inflicting great damage to the members of the community. Unfortunately we have not succeeded in putting a stop to his destructive behavior."

"He must have some merit," the Maggid insisted.

"Yes," the man replied. "He is a man of his word."

"Where can I find him?" the Maggid asked.

"Rebbe, I already told you that it is impossible to talk to him." Before he could continue a man appeared from the distance. "There he is! I am going to disappear, so that he has no idea who you were speaking to."

The Maggid turned to walk toward Yankel. With a bright smile, he reached out to greet him warmly. "Shalom Aleichem, *Reb Yaakov!*"

Yankele was rather shocked at the warm greeting. The Maggid continued: "I would like to ask you to do a small favor for me."

"I don't do favors," Yankele replied.

The maggid persisted, "Even so, Reb Yaakov ..."

Yankele was curious. "Nu, tell me what you want."

Encouraged, the Maggid continued: "You know that a maggid traditionally gives a lecture in the main shul and the listeners show their appreciation by throwing some coins into a plate. I am very poor, and I am convinced that if a well-known personality such as yourself comes to my lecture, others will follow your lead."

"I don't do any favors," Yankele bristled.

The Maggid did not give up begging Yankele to cooperate. Finally, Yankele said, more to get rid of him than to signal his commitment, "Okay. I'll come." With that he turned to leave.

The Maggid grabbed his arm saying, "Thank you. I heard you always keep your word." Yankele just nodded.

That Sunday, the shul was full. All eagerly awaited the visiting maggid. The Maggid did not start until he noted the arrival of Yankele. With *distaste, the Yidden cleared a path for the town slanderer as he made his way to the front of the shul. The* maggid *received him with warmth and gave him a sought-after spot on the eastern wall. The astonishment of those gathered knew no bounds. What did the righteous Maggid and the wicked slanderer have in common?*

The Maggid rose immediately and began to speak. He started by pointing out that every Jew has a portion in the World to Come. He elaborated on this theme and then explained how the Gates of Repentance are never locked. The Maggid was a gifted orator; his audience was riveted to their seats as he wove the simple and the complex into one mesmeric tapestry.

He then turned his attention to Yankele. "You too, Reb Yaakov! Don't think that you don't have a portion in the World to Come. It is entirely in your hands. If you think I am dreaming, I hereby announce before all of those gathered here today that I am ready to give you the reward for all my mitzvos and my portion in the World to Come, on condition you do teshuvah." He then briefly summarized his accomplishments up to that day.

He called the city's Dayanim *to come forward and prepare a document attesting to his sale of his Olam Ha'ba to Yankele. The Maggid signed it and handed it to Yankele, whose face shone with joy. He could not believe his good fortune — the Maggid's World to Come was now his.*

The Maggid was not finished with his lecture. Raising his voice to fire-and-brimstone intensity, he cited the words of the Gemara: *"These have no portion in the World to Come and are cut off, lost and destroyed for eternity because of their wickedness: nonbelievers and deniers ... those who slander their fellow Jews to the authorities."*

Turning to Yankele, he continued in a beseeching tone, "Remember Reb Yaakov! Remember, and don't lose you place in the World to Come. Don't associate with the goyim; turn over a new leaf, live a blissful life of Torah and fear of G-d! Do not destroy with your own hands the precious treasure you have acquired!"

The next day, the Maggid left town and continued on his way.

Seventeen years later he returned to Yankele's town. He asked the first person he met, "What happened to Yankel the Mossur?" The man had no idea who he was talking about. He added some more details until the man realized that the Maggid was referring to "Reb Yaakov the Tzaddik," the most spiritually elevated member of the community. Since the day of the Maggid's lecture he had not left the shul. He davened, studied, ate, and slept there. In the beginning, kind people taught him how to read and introduced him to the study of Torah. By now, he was an outstanding scholar; righteous women made sure that he had enough to eat. The Maggid's face took on a delighted glow!

He sent a message to the community leaders asking permission to give a lecture. At the appointed time everyone was present. Yankele sat in an inconspicuous place as befitting his newfound modesty and listened intently to every word the Maggid uttered.

The Maggid began with the words of the Mishnah in Yoma (85:2): "Sins against Hashem are forgiven on Yom Kippur but sins committed against one's fellow man are not atoned for on Yom Kippur until you appease your friend." He noted that even suffering and death cannot atone for this type of sin until one appeases one's friend.

The Maggid then turned to Yankele, addressing him with the following words: "You, formerly Yankele the Mossur, are now called Yaakov the Tzaddik. Do you remember how many people you oppressed and stole from? Do you recall the names of the widows and orphans you demoralized, the many people you brought down with your slander?

"How fearful is your lot! How dreadful your punishment! It would appear that the Gates of Repentance are closed before someone such as yourself, who was the cause of so much anguish. All the suffering in this world cannot possibly atone for a slanderer." Yankele dissolved into a pool of bitter sobs. His wailing moved all present to heartfelt tears.

After a few moments of respectful silence, the Maggid continued. "Let us try to come up with a way to help Yankele. The Shulchan Aruch advises that if a *person was not able to appease someone prior to the person's death, the proper procedure is to collect a minyan, go to the deceased's gravesite, and confess. Yankele however, does not even know whom he has hurt, so how can he do teshuvah? From whom will he ask for forgiveness? To whom will he return that which was stolen? I have only one suggestion. Here, in this holy convocation, with the entire community present, ask everyone for forgiveness. Let the new generation act on behalf of their parents who are no longer alive. Now Yankele, stand up and ask everyone for forgiveness, as instructed by our Sages, and they will reply three times, 'You are forgiven.'"*

Yankele had fainted from great emotion. When they revived him, he lacked the strength to walk to the bimah. He was carried on a chair. The Maggid opened the aron kodesh and told Yankele to repeat after him word for word, "I have sinned against the G-d of the Jews and citizens of this city."

The community as one responded with force, "You are forgiven! You are forgiven! You are forgiven!"

The Maggid rose and kissed Yankele on his forehead. "May baalei teshuvah such as you multiply among the Jewish people! Now you are truly worthy of the title 'Yankele the Tzaddik.'"

(Hizaharu Be'mamon Chaveireichem)

The Aderes writes: "Once I got into a dispute with my friend Rav Shlomo Arye Gurwitz and we didn't *speak to one another for quite some time. Then, on the night of* Yom Kippur, *I reminded myself that I must make* shalom *with him to receive his forgiveness, if I wanted to receive forgiveness from Hashem on* Yom Kippur. *So I went to his* beis medrash *and in front of his entire congregation, I asked him to forgive me. It was very embarrassing for me, but in my heart I felt an immense endless happiness."*

The Aderes adds: *"Every year during my* Shabbos Shuvah derashah, *I would ask forgiveness from the entire congregation in case I had ruled incorrectly (for example if I said a chicken wasn't kosher when it really was) or if I caused people to wait too long in line before I was able to answer their questions, or for other misdeeds or mistakes. I also announced that I forgive everyone in the congregation, and that no one need approach me to ask for forgiveness."*

(Aderes, Nefesh Dovid)

If a person cannot find the one he has wronged, he should try to encourage others to repent, to achieve atonement for his deeds. One way to do so is to encourage people to study the topic of teshuvah. (*Menoras Ha'maor*, Part 3, Candle 5) What can we do if asking forgiveness is impossible because we cannot trace the person we have hurt? Consider the following story:

Someone once told Rav Shlomo Zalman of Vilna a ridiculous chiddush *to which he expressed his disapproval in no uncertain terms.*

He immediately regretted having spoken so bluntly, but before he could ask for forgiveness, the man disappeared. Rav Zalman spent days searching for him, to no avail. He became ill with distress, and in order to alleviate his pain, his father-in-law had someone pretend to be the humiliated stranger and forgive him. Unfortunately, Rav Zalman immediately saw through the ruse and forced the man to admit that he was an imposter.

Rav Zalman's distress just increased. "What hope is there for me?" he moaned, shedding a flood of tears. "Even Yom Kippur *cannot atone for a sin like this until I appease the offended person."*

When the Vilna Gaon heard of his beloved student's distress, he sent for Rav Zalman and cited the gemara *where Rabbi Yehoshua ben Levi says that man's evil inclination rises up against him every day and seeks to take his life. As it says, "The wicked one waits for the tzaddik and seeks to kill him, and if the Holy One did not help him it would conquer him. As it says, 'Hashem will not leave him in his hands'"* (Tehillim 37:33) (Succah 52)

The Gaon continued, "The last part of this statement is telling us that more than Hashem's involvement is saving us from the yetzer hara*. It is also telling us that man's duty is simply to do all he can to fight the evil inclination, but once he has done his utmost, Hashem will grant him Heavenly assistance.*

"Hashem knows that you have done everything possible," the Gaon concluded. "Now He will send

> *His help, and he has several ways of returning people to the truth and good they are seeking."*
>
> *Opening* Chovos Ha'levavos, *the Gaon showed him a paragraph in Shaar Ha'teshuvah (chapter 10): "If a person did evil to his fellow, to his body or his property, the Creator will introduce willingness and love into his heart so that he forgives the one who sinned against him. As it says* (Mishlei 16:7): *When a man's ways please Hashem, even his enemies will make peace with him."*
>
> *Because Rav Zalman regarded every word the Gaon said as* ruach ha'kodesh, *he took comfort from the words and his cloud of misery dispelled.*

What do we do if the person we have sinned against is no longer alive? The *Gemara* advises that we take ten people to his grave and ask for his forgiveness (*Yoma* 77).

> *When Rav Yechezkel Avramsky was a young man, he visited a very old Rav. During the course of the visit, someone entered with a question and the Rav replied. Rav Yechezkel believed his answer to be incorrect, but out of respect for the Rav he remained quiet. The question did not relate to an obligation, but was a matter of custom. He reasoned that the honor of the Rav took precedence. After the questioners left, he continued talking to the Rav and managed to turn the conversation to the area of the* Shulchan Aruch *that discusses the issue he had just dealt with. The Rav realized that he had*

Asking Others for Forgiveness

erred and thanked Rav Yechezkel for pointing out his mistake.

Rav Yechezkel writes: "I parted with the Rav and went home. A while after returning to my hometown, my conscience began to bother me. Perhaps I caused the Rav anguish when I showed him the source in Shulchan Aruch? True, he had thanked me, but it might have hurt him to have such a young rabbi catch him making a mistake.

"Since his decision related only to a custom, and a Rav as old as he was would never likely encounter such a question again, I should have chosen not to react at all. I truly regretted my deed for I might have been guilty of humiliating the Rav. I decided to sit down and write a letter begging his forgiveness.

"Unfortunately, before I could pen the letter I was told that the Rav had passed away. I therefore took time to travel to the Rav's burial place to beg his pardon. I had a hard time getting ten people to join me at his grave. I had to pay them for their trouble. When they said 'You are forgiven' three times, I was able to return home."

(Peninei Rabbeinu Yechezkel 35)

Creating an environment of good will and understanding is an effective means of ensuring a good year.

It was the custom of Reb Menachem Mendel of Lubavitch, on the first night of Rosh Ha'shanah, *to deliver a discourse on Chassidus, followed by fiery words of inspiration to his chassidim.*

One year, when he had completed his discourse on the night of Rosh Ha'shanah, he turned to his chassidim and said, "Today we have to make ourselves ready to greet Him Whom we address in our prayers as 'Our Father, our King.' A father likes to see a pure heart; a king likes a clean garment."

Then Reb Menachem Mendel went on to explain that the Divine mission appropriate to the New Year season was for every person to purify his heart, and cleanse his "garments" — in thought, word, and deed.

"Every man is accompanied by two angels," he continued. "When, after the evening prayers of Rosh Ha'shanah, the angels hear each person sincerely wishing his neighbor, 'May you be inscribed and sealed for a good year,' they soar aloft and appear as defense attorneys in the Heavenly Court. There, they plead that the well-wishers be granted a good and a sweet year."

Reb Menachem Mendel concluded his own words with the blessing, "May you all be inscribed and sealed for a good year."

33
Shortcuts to Teshuvah

There are certain deeds that ensure that Hashem is more forgiving. When a person undertakes to forgive others for the wicked deeds perpetrated against him, Hashem more readily overlooks his own evil deeds (*Nidchei Yisroel* 35). Here are two areas to focus on in order to best prepare for the *Yom Ha'din*. The first is: deeds that cause the most harm to others. For example, one should be extra careful in business dealings with the poor, because any loss that a destitute person suffers hurts much more than an even-greater loss would wound a rich client.

The second area to concentrate on is: transgressions for which there will be the most punishment. How can one ascertain which those are? The concept of *"Le'fum tza'arah agrah"* teaches us that when we do something that is hard for us to do, our reward increases according to the difficulty. Rav Yisroel Salanter quotes the *gemara* in *Menachos* (43) which says, "The punishment for not having white [tzitzis] is greater than that of failing to have the blue [string]." The reason, Rashi explains, is that white is more available and easier to obtain.

The failure to do those mitzvos which are easy demonstrates greater indifference to the wishes of the King. Hence it carries greater punishment. Therefore, the majority of a person's punishment is due to ignoring those mitzvos which are easy to keep. At least during Elul, one must double one's efforts to be careful with mitzvos that are easily fulfilled but one is lax about. Teshuvah in these areas will exempt him from much of the punishment that would have been due to him.

The *Nidchei Yisroel* then explains a concept which is, on the one hand, extremely frightening, but, on the other hand, exuberantly encouraging. If someone ignores mitzvos which are easy for him to keep, then even sins which are difficult for him to avoid are judged as if they are easy, in other words, more stringently. This is because the verdict of the Heavenly Court is that even if they were easy, he would have succumbed to the *yetzer hara* and would have ignored them as well!

However, the opposite works in our favor. If he fulfills difficult mitzvos and avoids tempting *aveiros,* then, because he shows that he is a determined servant of Hashem, the Heavenly Court concludes that he certainly would have fulfilled the easy challenges even if they had been hard. Therefore his easy accomplishments are judged as if they had been difficult for him and thus his reward is enhanced many times.

It is well known that on *Rosh Ha'shanah* the righteous are immediately granted life and the wicked receive a verdict of death, while those in the middle have their sentences suspended until *Yom Kippur* (*Rosh Ha'shanah*

16b). The *Yerushalmi* in *Rosh Ha'shanah* (7a) says that if these *beinonim* do teshuvah, then they are included with the tzaddikim, but if not, then they are designated as wicked.

Even one who has not yet done teshuvah for ignoring easy mitzvos has hope. He should at least decide resolutely to learn *mussar* daily, since his *mussar* learning will motivate him and give him the tools to do teshuvah. The *Nidchei Yisroel* explains that because of Hashem's boundless love for us, He will view this resolution as if the person is doing teshuvah!

Food For Thought

It is said that Rav Simcha Zissel of Kelm studied the third section of *Shaarei Teshuvah* for three years (*Ha'meoros Ha'gedolim* #59). The Chofetz Chaim studied the *sefer* twice a week for an extensive period (ibid.; *Chofetz Chaim* #44)

It is a good idea to get a good teacher and a good friend to help guide you. You need someone to provide you with advice and a role model to measure yourself by. As you embark on the teshuvah process, you should ally yourself with a peer group that is preparing for *Yom Kippur* with the same intensity as you are. In prewar Europe, many great rabbis would spend the Ten Days of Repentance in the courts of the great Rebbes or in the great yeshivos. Reb Elchonon Wasserman would travel to Radin to prepare for *Yom Kippur* in the presence of the Chofetz Chaim. (*Reb Elchonon*)

The Study of *Mussar* and Teshuvah

The *mussar* authorities state that the only way we can come to a true realization of our status is to dedicate ourselves to serious study of *mussar*, which can reveal the real state of our being. Only the exhaustive and passionate study of *mussar* can reach our subconscious. After taking a personal inventory, a person will hopefully be motivated to institute the proper changes.

"It is of great importance for everyone to go to the *beis medrash* to hear the words of admonishment which are taught there. One who hates rebuke is very remote from teshuvah. As it says, 'Reproof is a friend to one who forsakes the path [of right]; one who hates rebuke will die' " (*Chayei Adam, Teshuvah*). A person who does not welcome rebuke will come to hate those who rebuke him. He will then begin to hate those who fulfill the word of Hashem, and ultimately their leaders as well. He will try to prevent others from doing mitzvos and even deny that the mitzvos originate with Hashem. From there it is only a short step to denying Hashem's existence, *Rachmana litzlan*. (*Sifra* on *Vayikra* 26)

The *Chayei Adam* advises that a person study daily those works which inculcate fear of G-d, for such study is vital. The *Yesod Ve'shoresh Ha'avodah* stresses the value of familiarizing oneself with the judgment and punishment that awaits a person who sins.

> **Food For Thought**
>
> Rav Chaim of Brisk attested that if an individual who was regarded as righteous did not study *mussar*, his virtue was questionable.
>
> (*Shimusha shel Torah* 102)

The author of the *Chavas Daas* pointed out that the study of *mussar* softens the heart (Last Will and Testament). Choose a *mussar sefer* that you feel an affinity for and is most suited to your temperament. The Chida recommended the study of *Reishis Chochmah*. (*Moreh Be'etzbah* 17) Reb Zundel of Salant preferred *Mesilas Yesharim*. *Shaarei Teshuvah* is singled out by the Chofetz Chaim. He recommends *Menoras Ha'maor* for women [in his famous letter on behalf of Sarah Schenirer]. Rav Yisroel Salanter states, in no uncertain terms, that no one is exempt from this type of study. Both men and women are obligated to study *mussar* (*Ohr Yisrael* 3).

Before beginning any shiur, the Chasam Sofer would teach a portion of Chovos Ha'levavos. He wanted to make sure that his students knew it well. He would also recommend that they study Menoras Ha'maor *on a regular basis. He was quick to point out that on a day he did not learn* mussar, *he felt his fear of Hashem waning.*

(Chut Ha'meshulash)

During the Ten Days of Repentance, Rav Yisroel Salanter allowed the study of mussar *to take up time usually devoted to the study of* Gemara *and* Poskim *because of its importance in preparing for* Yom Kippur *(according to Rav Naftali Amsterdam, as recorded in* Kisvei Ha'saba Mi'Kelm *74). The Chofetz Chaim, who advocated the study of* Chovos Ha'levavos, Shaarei Teshuvah, Orchos Tzadikkim, *and the like, added that sometimes it would take time until the person could actually feel the results of this study. Just as medications take time to take effect, so does the study of* mussar. *Also, just as one should not skip a day of medication, the study of these texts should not be neglected even one day. The Chofetz Chaim taught* Shaarei Teshuvah *in the yeshivah of Radin twice weekly.*

(Ha'meoros Ha'gedolim #129, 130, 189)

Rav Chaim Shmulevitz would often repeat a story about his father, Rav Alter Shmulevitz. When Rav Yeruchem Levovitz passed through Stutchin, before taking the position in Mir, Rav Alter asked him to stay and take charge of the spiritual development of the local yeshivah.

Rav Alter later admitted that he did not have money for a salary, but told him that he was ready to give the shirt off his back. Even though Stutchin didn't really need an additional mussar *lecturer, because the city's Rav was the great* mussar *personality Rav Leib Chasman, he was still ready to give the shirt off his back for an additional* shiur.

(Moreshes Avos 182)

Reb Boruch Ber of Kamenitz did not study mussar *regularly because of its dramatic impact on him. On one occasion, he was so profoundly affected by his study of* mussar *that he could not sleep all night, and the next day he was incapable of giving his* shiur. *(A similar story is told of Rav Nassan Wachtfogel.)*

(Ha'rav Domeh Le'malach 304)

The sefer Derech Chaim, *by Rabbi Dov Ber of Lubavitch (the Mitteler Rebbe), dealing in great length with the various levels of teshuvah and the way to attain them, had such a great effect on Reb Elchonon Dov Morozov that he would cry bitterly each time he studied it. Troubled by his intense crying, someone complained to the Rebbe Rashab. The Rebbe called for Reb Elchonon and forbade him to* study the sefer. However, the sefer had such an emotional impact on Reb Elchonon that he would burst into tears whenever he saw the cover.

(*Chassidic Portraits*, Elchonon Lesches)

Repeating the Teshuvah Process Again and Again

When we do teshuvah it is most difficult not to be struck by the disheartening thought: "Haven't I been here before? Didn't I stand in this same place last *Yom Kippur*, reciting the same words, beating my chest, and perhaps even shedding a few tears? Why bother working and striving to make myself a better person through Elul, when past experience has shown that, soon after *Yom Kippur*, I will go back to my old ways?"

Here we are, back again, seemingly unchanged from last year. We begin to question the very nature of our teshuvah. If, as it seems, the teshuvah process of previous years has had no lasting effect on us, then perhaps it wasn't teshuvah at all! Perhaps we are simply deluding ourselves; going through the motions, but lacking any true conviction. Certainly many people have, at some time, been struck by the above thoughts, sometimes almost to the point of debilitation.

> **Food For Thought**
>
> To those who grappled with this issue, the Chazon Ish would say, "Do you think it is an insignificant accomplishment to be close to Hashem for a few weeks?"
>
> (*Aleinu Le'shabeiach*, vol. VI, pp. 298–299)

We should always strive to think positively so that we don't set ourselves up for failure. It is likely that what appears like old challenges are highly nuanced variations of erstwhile challenges so that perforce, our reactions to them would have to be different. We must strive to the best of our ability to respond positively to all challenges while davening for the Heavenly guidance that we will be able to continue on our new path.

> **Food For Thought**
>
> By using the words "[Return, O Israel,] until Hashem," the prophet Hoshea is intimating that we will never quite achieve the objective. "Return to Hashem," would have implied that one is in fact capable of completing the journey. Returning *until* Hashem drives home the fact that teshuvah is a constant and ongoing process. Don't expect to ever "get there," yet never stop trying.
>
> (*Ksav Sofer*)

The prophet Hoshea recognizes the frustration a Jew might feel as he approaches Hashem for the umpteenth time, asking once again for forgiveness. He therefore offers us words of encouragement, reminding us that teshuvah is something we will spend our whole lives doing. We may never "make it," achieving absolute perfection, yet we will be far better Jews in the process.

Perhaps these are the "words" we are encouraged to "take with us" as we approach Hashem and ask Him to "forgive all iniquity, and take what is good." As long as we remain convinced that teshuvah is an "all-or-nothing" process in which we either succeed or fail, we will continue to be discouraged by our own imperfection and the roller coaster ride which is part of being human. In order to succeed in teshuvah, it is essential that we first recognize its nature.

Mayer was a descendant of Rav Yaakov Emden and had acquired a reputation for his sharp mind and penetrating insight. But, sadly, he began to stray from the path of the Torah. The holy Ruzhiner Rebbe, ztz"l, hearing of his errant ways, sent a messenger to Mayer in an attempt to convince him to return to a life of Torah and mitzvos. Yet he was reluctant. When the Rebbe promised to support him, Mayer agreed

One day, the Rebbe saw that Mayer was very distressed. "Why are you so sad? Is it because of your sins? But you have done teshuvah."

"Even after having done teshuvah," Mayer said to the Rebbe, "I am finding that it is to no avail, for I

keep succumbing to my evil desires. I have sadly concluded that I have strayed too far. For me, Rebbe, there is no hope."

"Since you were a yeshivah student," the Rebbe responded, "I will answer you with a scholarly explanation. We say in the Yom Kippur prayers, 'Ki Ata Salchan le'Yisrael — for You, Hashem, are the Forgiver of Israel.' Why do we refer to Hashem as a 'Salchan,' instead of the more familiar term 'Soleiach'?

"In parshas Mishpatim, we find the mitzvah of perikah — helping one's fellow unload his donkey. The Torah states (Shemos 23:5), 'If you will see the donkey of [even] your enemy crouching [roveitz] beneath its burden … you shall help him [unload]!" The Talmud [Bava Metzia 33a] comments on this verse: 'Roveitz, ve'lo ravtzan.' One must only assist in unloading if the donkey is roveitz [crouching] beneath its load, but not if it is a ravtzan.

"Rashi explains that roveitz means the animal is presently collapsing beneath its burden. But if the animal is a ravtzan — constantly and habitually overburdened — then there is no obligation to help unload it. From here we see that Hebrew suffix 'nun' after a verb signifies an act which is performed constantly or habitually.

"Now, since the holy Sages describe the Almighty as a Salchan, and not as a Soleiach," concluded the Rizhiner, "we have proof that Hashem constantly forgives us; there is no limit to how many times He will forgive our sins. Don't give up — it's never too late!" His words captured the heart of the young man, and he returned wholeheartedly to Torah and mitzvos for the rest of his life.

(*Mi'gedolei Ha'chassidus*, page 78)

> ### Inspiration
>
> Rabbi Avrohom Chayun questions whether a person who sinned, repented, and sinned again is considered to have repeated a sin or committed the sin for the first time. He decides that it depends on the way it is repeated. If he sins again while regretting having done teshuvah, then his original sin is not expiated. However, if he sins only because his passion overcame him and he wished that he had not succumbed, his original teshuvah remains in effect and only the second transgression lingers. (*Chomas Anach*)

Rav Mattisyahu Salomon tells about the Mir Yeshivah's amazing Yom Kippur *in Shanghai, China, during World War II. The davening was unbelievable. It was higher and purer than those of the years before. Rav Salomon related that in order to encourage his students, Rav Yechezkel (Chatzkel) Levenstein, the saintly* Mashgiach, *spoke at the end of the fast.*

He explained that he felt that the prayers and repentance were sincere and complete. Rav Chatzkel continued, "However, many of you are thinking that this moment of inspiration will pass. Tomorrow, we will slip from the high place onto which we have climbed today. So did we accomplish anything? What was the use? Let me tell you a story.

"There was once a man who built himself a beautiful mansion. He decided that during the celebration on finishing the mansion, he would climb up and place a beautiful ornament on the pinnacle of the roof.

"The great day came when he finished his mansion, and he made a special celebration and invited all his friends and family.

"The moment came when he climbed up to the roof to place the beautiful ornament. But just at that moment, a sudden gust of wind blew him off the roof. He dropped the ornament and fell to the ground. Dazed and in agony, he cried out, 'Oy, my mansion has fallen down. My mansion has fallen down.'

"His friends and family reassured him, 'Your mansion hasn't fallen down. You have. You may have broken bones and have to go the hospital. But when you recover, the mansion will still be there. You'll be able to go into it. It hasn't fallen down.' "

Rav Chatzkel concluded, "My dear children, we built a mansion this Yom Kippur. Every prayer that we offered is like a different room, and all together *we have constructed a beautiful mansion. If tomorrow we feel that we have lost some of our inspiration, I want you to know that the mansion hasn't fallen down. It will be we that have fallen down. The mansion will still be standing. It will stand forever.*

Rabbi Salomon reflected on these words: "Rav Chatzkel's words of encouragement to his students in the heat of a world war are an important lesson to all of us. When we stand in the shul and prepare to pray to G-d, the thought can sometimes be so intimidating that we may lose heart. We know that it will take so much emotional and spiritual effort to reach the highest level of prayer to which we aspire. Who knows if we will be successful? And even if we are, we will be able to maintain ourselves on that high level? Or will we fall back to earth, so to speak? And if we do, is all the effort worthwhile?

One day, we will enter our mansion once again. When and how, that depends on us, but the mansion will always be there waiting for us. It will be there forever.

(*With Hearts Full of Faith*, pg. 103–104)

Yetzer Hara's Deterrent to Teshuvah

When a person makes up his mind to return to Hashem, the *yetzer hara* immediately steps in. A person who is reluctant to struggle with his *yetzer hara* will find that personal refinement is impossible. The *yetzer hara* may begin by throwing a blanket of complacency over us with his suggestion that serious teshuvah is for those who do gross sins. After all, we are careful to put on tefillin and to daven, and we try to say our blessings properly. We are careful not to hurt others, etc. Those who are constantly learning feel even more confident in the face of the upcoming judgment.

When a certain Rosh Yeshivah met a neighbor before *Rosh Ha'shanah* and gave him a *beracha* that he should merit doing proper teshuvah, the neighbor was very insulted. He said to the Rav, "What have I done wrong? I am a *frum* Jew who is careful to keep all the mitzvos as Hashem commanded. Why then does the Rav say to me that I must do teshuvah?"

If Shmuel Ha'navi trembled at the possibility of being called for judgment, how much more should *we* tremble as

Rosh Ha'shanah approaches? (*Chagigah* 4b; see commentaries on *Shmuel I* 28) Haven't we heard of the suffering which even the great ones among us endure?

Do we also have our heads buried in the sand? Are we oblivious to the fact that so many of the mitzvos we do are performed mechanically or driven by the wrong motivations? We should be distressed at disappointing our Creator, Who is, as it were, standing and waiting for even one small fleeting moment of sincerely offered repentance.

Inspiration

The Baal Ha'tanya develops quite vividly, with a parable, the concept of the joy inherent in closeness to Hashem: "Imagine two people standing very close to one another, but back-to-back. Although they are physically close, there is no greater distance than this.

"Teshuvah can be understood in the same way. The prophet Yechezkel says, 'They faced me with the back of their necks.' This is surprising. How can the back of their necks be termed 'facing'? The answer is that they were fulfilling the mitzvos — this is the meaning of the term 'facing.' However, they did it without love, without enthusiasm, just going through the motions. This is the symbolism of 'the back of the neck,' which shows a lack of emotion. The meaning of 'they faced me with the back of their necks,' is that they did the mitzvos, but coldly, without *simchah*.

"We see teshuvah, then, in a new light. Teshuvah is to 'turn back' so that we are 'face-to-face' with Hashem —

> that is to transform our inner selves into vehicles of love and desire for His Torah and mitzvos in a joyous and generous spirit."
>
> (*Likutei Torah, parshas Acharei Mos*)

Alternatively, the *yetzer hara* might try the tactic of pointing out that last year we didn't go through serious repentance, and yet we had a good year. But this may be because the merits of our parents was protecting us. Or deferment of our punishment could be because our cup of sins is not full. Why was the city of Sodom destroyed while the city of Tzoar — equally as wicked — was spared? Tzoar was granted a reprieve because it was built one year later and therefore the total of its sins was fewer (*Omek Ha'din*). The fact that Hashem is long-suffering should increase our anguish at the mountain of sins we have created (*Menoras Ha'maor*, Candle Five).

When all else fails, the *yetzer hara* insists that, "If you want to repent you must do so completely, from the bottom of your heart, with absolutely pure intentions, and no ulterior motives." But he quickly lets us know that we are incapable of doing that, since we are so blemished. He raises the ante just high enough that it appears insurmountable, blocking all access to teshuvah. This is only one of the multitudes of psychological tricks that he has at his beck and call.

The *yetzer hara* is sure to remind us of our many sins, character flaws, and bad habits. He is at our side, citing a hundred clear proofs from the Torah and *Gemara* that we can no longer repair what we have damaged, neither in our relationship to Hashem nor to our fellow men. (Rav Yaakov Meir Shechter) In short, he soon has us believing that we have strayed too far, to a point of no return, *Rachmana litzlan*, and that our waywardness has precluded any possibility of teshuvah. He crushes us with the impression that we can never turn back and make amends. (*Imrei Noam, parshas Metzorah*) This is the equivalent of forcefully pushing us from the back *into* transgression and then blocking our return.

A person who believes that he is distant from Hashem and that his actions are not important to Hashem because they are not pure and whole, could really distance himself, *chas ve'shalom*, to no end." (*Daas Zekeinim, Baalei Tosfos, Vayikra* 2:13; *Emes Ve'emunah* 85)

Inspiration

Rabbi Shimon bar Yochai says: "Do not consider yourself a *rasha*." The Rambam elaborates that this will lead one to associate with evil company, because he then gives up all hope of improving — which is merely another tactic of the *yetzer hara*.

(*Pirkei Avos* 2:13)

Rav Yechezkel Landau of Prague, the Noda B'Yehudah, had a student who became an apostate and then repented. The student later revealed what had caused him to stray from the path of Torah. One Shabbos, a question arose as to the kashrus of the kugel being served in the household where this student was eating. The young man was asked to take the kugel to the Rav of the city to ascertain if it could be eaten. After inspecting the kugel, the Rav told him that although the kugel was kosher, anyone meticulous about the fulfillment of mitzvos should not eat it.

This student loved kugel. Instead of relaying this ruling to his host, he ate the whole kugel himself. When he arrived back at his host's, he told the family that the Rav had ruled that the kugel was forbidden, and he had therefore disposed of it.

The student was suddenly overcome with guilt; he had lied, stolen, and eaten something which he should have refrained from eating. How could he have allowed himself to be overcome by such a fleeting temptation?

That night, the student could not sleep. Dreams of his unworthiness plagued him. When he awoke in the morning, he didn't even wash negel vasser, *feeling he would be a hypocrite if he was particular about that halachah, when he had sullied his mouth.*

It was all downhill from there. No negel vasser *led to no berachos, no davening, no tefillin, and no Shabbos; shortly afterwards, he left Yiddishkeit altogether for Christianity.*

(Adapted from *You Can Make the Difference*, pg. 39–40)

Despair is a prime tool of the *yetzer hara* to quell thoughts of repentance that enter our heart. There is no such thing as having gone too far away. We need only look around us: many of the *baalei teshuvah* we know turned their life upside down for Hashem's sake. Their revolutionary transformation makes our required makeovers appear simple to the extreme. If teshuvah helped those with numerous sins erase the past and start anew, it can certainly help those with fewer sins. If we're not convinced, we should just get started. We are not obligated to complete the task, but we must begin (*Avos* 2:16).

Food For Thought

Hashem has promised that He will uphold the Thirteen Middos of Compassion. The first two of G-d's Names refers to his compassion before we sin and His compassion after we have repented.

(*Rosh Ha'shanah* 17:2)

Hashem's compassion stands ready to assist us (Ramban's introduction to *Chumash Devarim*). Hashem is referred to in our prayers as a Forgiver. He will forgive again and again, as long as one's teshuvah is sincere.

(Ruzhiner Rebbe)

One of the biggest obstacles to changing is the belief that we are unable to change or improve. To change we must be convinced that change is possible. Rabbeinu Yonah advises that we should view ourselves as if we were a newborn baby, starting life over again. The belief in our ability to live life on a much higher level than before will engender relief. Secure in Hashem's forgiveness, it is then possible to contend with the *yetzer hara*. We must ignore the inner voice that tells us that it is impossible to rectify our sins. It is well known that there may be a worthy act that equals several sins and a sin that equals several worthy deeds. (*Hilchos Teshuvah* of the Rambam) This thought should offer a measure of reassurance in our battle with the *yetzer hara*.

Inspiration

Rav Isaac expounded that the Holy One, blessed be He, said to Yirmiyahu, "Go and urge the Jews to repent." But when Yirmiyahu came to the Jews with that demand, they complained, "How can we repent after we have annoyed and enraged Hashem with our idolatry, and while those mountains and hills where we have worshipped the idols are still standing upright and remind us of our shame?" Yirmiyahu reported this complaint to the Holy One, blessed be He, whereupon He retorted, "Go and tell them this: to Who is it that you return? Is it not to your all-merciful Father in Heaven?"

(*Pesikta Rabbasi* 28)

> Even when the Jews sin, Hashem tries to save them by all the means at His disposal. That is what happened in the days of Yirmiyahu. As it says, "Run to and fro through the streets of Yerushalayim and see now, and know and seek in the broad places thereof, if you can find a man, if there be any, who does justly, who seeks truth — and I will pardon him."
>
> (*Yirmiyahu* 5:1)

Some people avoid repentance because they believe they will never be able to maintain their righteousness over a long period. The Ohr Ha'chaim writes that he met wicked people who told him they really would like to improve. If they knew they would die immediately after they repented, they would repent. But they feared they would not be able to behave in the improved manner for more than a short time. Therefore they totally despaired of changing. (*Bamidbar* 23)

In truth, even a small amount of improvement for a short time is worthwhile. Even if the resolution is ultimately abandoned, we are rewarded for every moment of teshuvah. In a military battlefield, total victory is all that matters, but in battles of the spirit, Hashem enjoys the struggles — especially when we do not lose hope. Every Jew has within him a "spark" that draws him to Hashem. In many people, this spark is covered by many layers and may be almost inaccessible. Yet it is always there, waiting to be ignited by some stirring of conscience to become a better person.

37

Sincere Teshuvah

Reb Simcha Bunim of Peshischa wonders why the sin of the Golden Calf was forgiven, even though the Jewish people did not do teshuvah, whereas the Sin of the Spies, where we find *Bnei Yisroel* doing teshuvah — as it says, "And the people moaned deeply" (*Numbers* 14:39) — they were not forgiven.

He explains that if a man knows that he has no hope at all and nevertheless this man burns inside to serve Hashem from now on, no matter what, this is true repentance. After the sin of the Golden Calf, the Jews did just that. It was their first transgression and they had no direct knowledge of the power of teshuvah to secure Divine pardon. They put themselves at the mercy of Hashem.

The second time around, after the Sin of the Spies, they already knew the effectiveness of teshuvah and they hoped to take advantage of that option as they had once before. This ulterior motive diminished the purity of their teshuvah, which was not nearly as passionate, enfeebling its success. (*Ohel Torah* 95)

> *The descendants of Sisra, Sancheriv, and Haman, became Torah scholars. Rav Mayer was a descendant of the Caesar Nero.*
>
> (*Gittin*)

The Shelah writes: "There is nothing standing in the way of teshuvah. Even if one committed all the sins under the sun, he may repent. Ha'kadosh Baruch Hu welcomed even the teshuvah of Menashe, who erected an idol in the *Heichal* and committed all sorts of other sins. Similarly, Yeravam ben Nevat sinned and incited the public (against Hashem), but if he had returned, Hashem would have accepted his teshuvah. This is what is said in *Chagiga*: "A heavenly echo cries out, 'Return you wayward sons, except for Acher.'" Had Acher begged and pleaded, multiplying prayer, mortifying his flesh with harsh suffering as Menashe did, he might have earned great mercy. Even though he heard the Heavenly comment, "except for Acher," he should not have spared any effort in seeking mercy.

Dovid Ha'melech likened the teshuvah process to the distance between east and west: "As far as east is from west has He distanced our transgressions from us" (*Tehillim* 103:12). Why does Dovid Ha'melech use east to west as a basis of comparison rather than north to south. If a person stands at a given point and wants to travel north, he will be northbound until he reaches the North Pole. If he continues walking past the North Pole, he will be traveling south. The same is true for someone traveling south. He will be southbound until he hits the South Pole. Thereafter he will be traveling north. But if a person travels east, he can travel as long as pleases but his direction won't ever change. He will continue to travel eastward. The only way for him to change direction is by making an about face, turning towards the west. Dovid Ha'melech teaches us that just as the distance between east and west is only one action (a 180-degree turn), so too can we walk away from our transgressions just by the one action of turning around.

Certain dramatic actions are the equivalent of a 180-degree turn. Rav Yisroel Salanter, *ztz"l*, writes that it is possible for a person to completely change his nature in a moment. An example of this is readily found by Rabbi Elazar ben Durdiyah:

> *Elazar ben Durdiyah indulged his every physical desire. He was told by a woman that he was so depraved that he could never do teshuvah. This so affected him that he begged the mountains and hills to pray for him. They replied, "Before we pray for you, we first must pray for ourselves."*
>
> *He then approached the heavens and the earth and asked them to pray for him. They likewise replied, "Before we pray for you, we first must pray for ourselves." He approached the sun and the moon, then the stars and constellations, but they all replied, "Before we pray for you, we first must pray for ourselves."*
>
> *Finally he said, "I now see that I must rely on myself." He realized that he was the only one responsible for his fate. He put his head between his knees and wept with such force that his soul left him.*

> *So great was his teshuvah that a Heavenly voice declared, "Rabbi Elazar Ben Durdiyah has entered the World to Come" (Avodah Zarah 17a).*
>
> (Those Who Returned, page 187)

Elazar ben Durdiyah's return to Hashem was so intense and he reached such a spiritual level that the title "Rabbi" was added to his name by Heaven.

According to the Maharsha, fearing that he would die, Elazar ben Durdiyah approached the mountains to intervene on his behalf so that he would not suffer the loss of This World. They replied that he ought not to be concerned about forfeiting This World, for the stuff of This World is transitory. They assured him that acquiring his place in the World to Come was far more significant. (Maharsha, *Avodah Zarah* 17a)

> *One of the students at Children's Town in Yerushalayim was an only child of totally secular parents. The boy suffered a great deal because he could not eat at home or spend Shabbos with his parents. Finally he managed to persuade his parents to kasher their kitchen. However, nothing else changed.*
>
> *Two years after the boy had become fully committed, his father appeared at Children's Town on the day before Shavuos.*
>
> *"Father! What are you doing here?" the boy asked in astonishment.*
>
> *His father replied, "It's been thirty years since I've been in a shul. I decided to come and see how Shavuos is celebrated here."*

He was up all night with those studying in the beis medrash *and in the morning he joined the yeshivah boys when they said* Tehillim. *They began with Chapter 119, repeating each verse aloud. When they got to the last verse, "I have strayed like a lost sheep; seek Your servant [bring him back to You] for your commandments I have not forgotten," the boy's father fainted.*

When he was revived, he began to sob, exclaiming again and again, "I have strayed like a lost sheep! I have strayed like a lost sheep!"

(*Sheal Avicha Ve'yagedcha*, pg. 134)

38

Teshuvah and Redemption

Teshuvah brings redemption to the world. Redemption can be defined as freedom from the *yetzer hara* with a heart committed to the service of Hashem (see *Nesivos Olam*). Teshuvah entrenches in our hearts the concept that Hashem is our G-d and none other (Rav Moshe of Kobrin). When a person repents he or she moves closer to this goal, which will only become a total reality with the coming of *Moshiach*. Rav Yisroel Salanter said that when one person does teshuvah, his thoughts and deeds have an impact on others, enabling others to make greater spiritual commitments (see *Tzidkas Ha'tzaddik* 159; *Takanas Ha'shavim* 70). That is why even when one person does teshuvah he and the entire world are forgiven. He purifies the environment, enabling Hashem's compassion to flow freely and making it easier for humanity to move towards the goal of bringing *Moshiach*.

There were many times in history when repentance could have resulted in redemption if it had been powerful enough. The Chofetz Chaim explains, with the following parable, how we ought to proceed:

A merchant placed a large order with the wholesaler with whom he often did business. The wholesaler filled the order and presented the merchant with a bill. The merchant asked the supplier for an extension of credit, because he was short of cash. The wholesaler was inclined to agree, until he looked up the merchant's credit record and saw that he already owed a large amount and had been derelict in his payments for a long time. The buyer offered various excuses as to why he had been unable to keep his word in the past, but he promised that this time he would remit payment as soon as he got home. He started to cry and plead to the wholesaler to have compassion on him and his family.

Being a goodhearted soul, the wholesaler considered giving in to the merchant's entreaties. But then his credit manger intervened and insisted that no further credit be extended. "This fellow owes us thousands of dollars! He never pays and his word is worthless! How can you think of giving him credit on another large order?!" the credit manger asked incredulously. The merchant hardened his heart and firmly insisted that the man pay cash up front.

A passerby, hearing the raised voices, was drawn inside. When he understood what was going on, he made a suggestion. Turning to the wholesaler, he said, "Although you normally sell in large quantities, why don't you make an exception for this gentleman? Sell him a small amount, and when he pays for that you can sell him a little more," he suggested.

"With the goods purchased, he would earn enough to come back and make another order. In this way, over time he would be able to pay off the debt in small increments."

Even at this suggestion, the credit manger balked. He pointed out that the man would no longer be purchasing enough to entitle him to wholesale prices. At that, the first merchant again started begging that he at least be able to continue buying at wholesale prices. The kind-hearted wholesaler agreed. With new resolve, the merchant went about building up his business, and over the course of a few years, working steadily yet slowly, he was able to pay off his whole debt. The arrangement worked well for both of them. Ultimately, the buyer managed to buy the entire amount that he had originally desired, and to make a large profit.

It is exactly the same with us, writes the Chofetz Chaim. We are constantly begging Hashem to send us *Moshiach*, for we no longer have the strength to endure all the suffering of this existence. And we promise that we will correct all that needs to be corrected. Hashem, in turn, answers that He is ready to send *Moshiach* if we repent properly. For Hashem reminds us that we have promised many times that if we are saved we will repent, and we never keep our word. (*Beis Yisroel*, pg. 10–11)

Even if Hashem were ready to acquiesce, the power of judgment prevents such action. We have no choice but to do teshuvah by gradually building up our spirituality. We invest effort in correcting our thoughts, correcting our speech, and correcting our deeds in a methodical fashion, so that our repentance is comprehensive. We can rest assured that we will succeed.

> ## INSPIRATION
>
> "And Hashem said to Moshe, 'Why do you cry to Me? Speak to *Bnei Yisroel*, that they go forward; lift up your staff and stretch out your arm over the sea and split it, and let *Bnei Yisroel* go on dry ground through the middle of the sea'" (*Shemos* 14:15–16).
>
> The Kotzker Rebbe believed that these verses were being directed to the tzaddikim who beseech Hashem to send *Moshiach* in a hurry. Doesn't Hashem want *Moshiach* to come? The real task is to cry out to Yisroel that they do *teshuvah*. Now we can understand what Hashem said to Moshe: "Why do you cry out to Me?" I want to hurry the Redemption. But first you must "speak to the Children of Yisroel that they go forward," leaving behind such wicked thoughts as when they asked you, "Weren't there any graves in *Mitzrayim* that you had to take us out to die in the wilderness?" (*Shemos* 14:11). Let them strengthen themselves in faith, and I will come to their aid.
>
> (*Lahavos Kodesh* 40)

The Ramban believes that the verse, "You will return to Hashem Your G-d" (*Devarim* 30:2), is both a mitzvah and a promise. The *Oznaim Le'torah* emphasizes that it is a definitive promise. In the end of our exile, the Jewish people will do teshuvah and they will be redeemed. The Torah has promised that Israel will do teshuvah — at the end of its exile — and will be redeemed immediately. As it says (*Devarim* 30): "It will be when all these things have happened ... you will return to Hashem ... and Hashem will return your captivity and will gather you from among all the nations where He dispersed you." *(Rambam, Hilchos Teshuvah)*

39
Teshuvah and *Simchah*

It would seem, at first glance, that the concept of *simchah* is the converse of teshuvah, which is rooted in *yirah* (fear). It is true that the teshuvah process is tied together with heartbroken remorse. But it is also true that a person should feel joy at having recognized that he sinned and that he is rectifying the matter. This is what Yosef was referring to when he told his brothers not to allow their great remorse to dominate their return trip. As they were dealing with these intense feelings, they needed to be reminded that it was imperative that they remain joyous. (Rabbeinu Yonah, *Igeres Ha'teshuvah* 13)

In reality, the chamber of teshuvah is a joyous place. The possibility of teshuvah generates hope, faith, and confidence. The joyousness in a heart that is firm and certain that Hashem desires to show kindness, and is gracious and compassionate, generously forgiving the instant one pleads for His forgiveness and atonement, is an amazing thing. Not the faintest vestige of doubt dilutes this absolutely blissful conviction. (*Ohr Rav Simchah Zissel*)

Imagine the joy of a person who found a lost, priceless heirloom after years of searching. His joy knows no bounds. Our joy is linked to Hashem's joy. When a person who is truly wicked does teshuvah, he is like the lost item, being restored to Hashem. Of course there is great joy in the discovery. (*Otzar Mishlei Chassidim* 110)

> *Once, while walking by Rav Yechezkel Levenstein's room during a break in the* Yom Kippur *davening, Rav Don Segal heard him singing parts of the* Yom Kippur *prayers in an inspiring joyous manner. This was typical of Rav Yechezkel's approach, for he taught that while one must have heartfelt fear of Heaven on* Yom Kippur, *one must also trust that Hashem will be merciful to him, and thus he sang.*
> (Reb Chatzkel, pg. 311)

Food For Thought

Rav Yitzchok Hutner noted: "*Yirah* and *simchah* mixed together is a concept known only to Jews. The trembling of *yirah* and the enthusiasm of *simchah* together create the taste of Yiddishkeit."

(*Sefer Ha'zikaron Le'baal Pachad Yitzchok* 102)

Just as all mitzvos must be fulfilled with *simchah*, so too the mitzvah of teshuvah should be marked by great joy (Rav

Aharon of Belz, *Ha'machaneh Chareidi*). The closeness to Hashem, which is the goal of teshuvah out of love, can only be achieved through *simchah*.

> *The Rebbe of Kobrin was asked why people say that* chazzanim *are foolish. He answered that it is well known that the Chamber of Neginah is near the Chamber of Repentance. When the* chazzan *sings, he is transported to the world of song. Why doesn't he slip into the Chamber of Complete Teshuvah. Can one imagine something more foolish than that?*
> (*Otzar Pisgamim Ve'sichos* 100)

Rav Avigdor Miller once told someone that being happy is an effective way to gain favorable judgment on *Rosh Ha'shanah*. He would cite the analogy of a business in which an employee whose performance is lacking is nonetheless valued by his employer, since his cheerful demeanor attracts many customers.

Joy is also a necessary result of the act of repentance. For every step away from sin is a step closer to virtue. Every move away from the darkness of evil is a move closer to the light of goodness, coming ever closer to Hashem. This fact must fill the heart with joy, a true and encompassing joy and happiness, even as the lost child rejoices in having found the way home. Indeed, this deep sense of joy, filling one's whole being, is the very test and proof of sincere teshuvah.

> *Rav Yechiel Danziger of Alexander would stress that a person ought to always be joyous, for*

joyousness drives away the yetzer hara. *He would cite the Baal Ha'tanya, who said that if a person is feeling low and suddenly feels the need to repent, this thought does not come from a good source. The* yetzer hara *is trying to lead a person to depression. It is imperative that we resist any thoughts of inadequacies. Forget whether we davened enough, or did enough* chessed, *or learned enough Torah. The important thing is to achieve a state of happiness. We must embrace joy; only then will we be able to do complete teshuvah.*

(Mi'gedolei Ha'torah)

Rabbi Ben Zion Abba Shaul took time out from his busy schedule to speak to a baal teshuvah *who appeared to be weighed down by the low level of his mitzvah observance. He explained to the young man that a Jew must fulfill his mitzvos with joy. He admitted that in his youth he was once extremely frazzled regarding the proper baking of his matzos. But when he saw his father's matzos, which were not nearly as presentable as his, and observed his father's great joy at doing the mitzvah properly, he realized that his approach was all wrong. Every aspect of every mitzvah should be performed with joy.*

He showed the young man that the daily toll of obligatory mitzvos was not large at all. All the other mitzvos that he voluntarily pursued could be completed at his convenience or only fulfilled partially.

> *The important thing was that he rejoice in the closeness to Hashem resulting from each mitzvah.*
> *(Chacham Rav Ben Zion Abba Shaul, pg. 74–75)*

Sinning can be viewed as a disgrace which can become reshaped into a vehicle steering us upwards. When teshuvah is viewed as bringing the person to a higher level, it is patently clear that teshuvah should never be a viewed as a burden.

> *A sinner once came to the tzaddik Rav Mordechai of Lechowitch and after confessing all his sins, asked for a way to repent. The Rebbe asked him if he would do anything he was told, and after receiving the sinner's full consent, he said, "You must not carry out any penance, but on the contrary, eat and drink of the best and finest foods and sleep on the softest bed for a whole year. When the year is over come to me again, and I shall see what you ought to do."*
>
> *The astonished man was puzzled at this advice and was sure that his sins would not be atoned for in such a manner. But since he had promised to carry out the Rebbe's words to the letter, he ate and drank as liberally as he could. But these indulgences gave him no pleasure, since his conscience kept bothering him. He would keep saying to himself, "Shame on you for enjoying yourself when you have sinned so much! A diet of dust and ashes would be more fitting!"*
>
> *The man grew thinner and more anguished every day. At year's end, when he came to the Rebbe again,*

he could hardly be recognized. The Rebbe saw his true remorse, realized that his instructions had achieved their aim, and told him to stop. He then told him how to conduct himself in an ordinary way, and the man eventually became renowned for his saintliness.

(Mipi Chassidim)

Reb Shmuel Munkis was a great man, a Lubavitcher chassid, known for his humor and wit. Reb Shmuel's greatness was recognized by all. Even the gentiles considered him a holy man. When they noticed that those fields where Reb Shmuel meditated yielded a bountiful harvest, the gentile farmers tried to find ways to get Reb Shmuel to come to pray in their fields.

During Elul, a maggid (traveling preacher) came to Reb Shmuel's town. The townspeople saw his letter of introduction, which referred to him as a great tzaddik who gave up his own comfort to travel from town to town, only to arouse and inspire Jews. Being G-d-fearing people, they immediately invited him to speak and inspire them to serve G-d better.

The maggid began his speech. Over and over again, he accused his audience of committing terrible sins. His entire speech was filled with accusations and descriptions of the terrible punishments awaiting them because their evil behavior had aroused G-d's anger. Only if they would wholeheartedly repent would they possibly have a chance to be spared. The townspeople were utterly broken by the maggid's harsh words, and they cried bitterly, fearing the awesome punishment due them.

After his speech, the maggid, satisfied with himself, retired to the room that the community had arranged for him.

A short while later, Reb Shmuel entered the maggid's room. He carried with him a long knife and a stone with which to sharpen it. Reb Shmuel closed the door behind him and then bolted it. Without saying a word, Reb Shmuel began to sharpen his knife.

A few tense moments passed. Finally the maggid broke the silence and asked in astonishment, "Sir, could you please tell me what you are doing?"

Without glancing up from the knife he was sharpening, Reb Shmuel answered, "As the honorable, great maggid knows, we are very simple people in this town. Perhaps, it is because of our unintentional sins that we have never merited having a great, righteous, G-d-fearing scholar in our midst."

Not knowing what to make of this answer, the maggid replied, "Yes, that is true. Nevertheless, what does that have to do with sharpening the knife?"

Reb Shmuel answered simply, "We were taught by our parents that before Rosh Ha'shanah, one is supposed to pray at the graves of the righteous."

Still unsure of what Reb Shmuel's point was, the maggid asked, "That is correct. But why are you sharpening that knife?"

"Oh, that is very simple," explained Reb Shmuel. "The nearest gravesite of a righteous person is very far from our town. For some of us it is extremely troublesome and difficult to make such a long journey."

With these additional words, the maggid began to feel uneasy. He started sweating and ventured, "But you still have not explained why you are sharpening your knife in this room!"

Reb Shmuel answered, "Quite simply, I am sharpening my knife here because the townspeople want a very righteous person buried in this town."

Now the maggid had not even a shadow of a doubt as to what Reb Shmuel's intentions seemed to be. The maggid stammered, "But I am not completely righteous. I have also done some small sins, such as ..."

Reb Shmuel dismissed the maggid's revelation, saying, "Honored maggid, you are still a very righteous and learned person. As for the sins that you mentioned, I did not even know that they were transgressions."

The maggid trembled and stuttered, "But I did some transgressions that were much more serious, such as ..."

Concerning this revelation, as well, Reb Shmuel shrugged, arguing, "But to us you are still a tzaddik; for us, you are quite good enough."

This strange dialogue continued for some time with the maggid mentioning more and more severe transgressions and Reb Shmuel telling him, "But you *are still acceptable to us, since you are far better than we are.*"

Finally, the maggid *admitted to some extremely serious transgressions and that he was not really the great tzaddik that his letter of introduction and credentials claimed him to be. In essence, he was saying, "I am an impostor."*

Now, Reb Shmuel no longer played the simpleton. After putting away the knife, he began chastising the maggid *for causing the Jews of the town so much pain and sorrow. After making sure the* maggid *fully understood how one is to talk to and treat another Jew, Reb Shmuel unbolted the door and let the* maggid *go on his way, much the wiser and more sensitive than before.*

(Early Chassidic Personalities:
Reb Shmuel Munkis, *by Rabbi S. D. Avtzon*)

A group of Ponovezh students visited the Chazon Ish on the first night of Rosh Ha'shanah, *to wish him a good year. The Chazon Ish responded in kind. One of the boys asked the Chazon Ish to give him a blessing and the Rav responded, "Ke'sivah ve'chasimah tovah." The boy was not satisfied: "Rebbe, I need a good blessing," he said. The Chazon Ish replied, "Aren't wishes for a* ke'sivah ve'chasimah tovah *a good blessing? What could be better than that?"*

The Chazon Ish realized that the fear of Judgment weighed heavily on the boy so he said, "Do you leave the synagogue, they drop a few coins into the containers. The larger or busier the shul, the more noise is made by the clanging and jingling of the coins as they are dropped in. And, of course, during these solemn days, more charity than usual is given.

> *In the Baal Shem Tov's shul, there was constant noise from the rattling of coins, so much so that some of the people found their prayers sorely disturbed. One person approached the Baal Shem Tov and asked him if it might be possible to abandon this disruptive custom.*
>
> *"Heaven forbid!" cried the Baal Shem Tov in horror. "It is this very jingling and clanging of the coins that is our deliverance during these awesome days. It confuses the Adversary on High who is trying to convince the Almighty that we are not worthy of being forgiven."*

The Baal Ha'tanya suggests that the prohibition of distributing more than one fifth of one's income to charity applies only to a perfectly righteous person, who needs to give charity only for the sake of fulfilling the mitzvah of *tzedakah*. But if a person has tainted himself with iniquity and his soul is afflicted with the malady of sin, then he must give *tzedakah* lavishly, in order to cure his soul. Doesn't a person suffering from a physical ailment spend all of his money to find a cure?

The Sanzer Rav could not get to sleep until every coin in his house was distributed among the poor. He could not relate to the wealthy having strongboxes in which they saved their money. His response was, "How can they sleep at night?"

The Sanzer Rav's son once gently reminded him that the halachah dictates that one should not give away more than one fifth of his assets to tzedakah.

The Sanzer Rav explained, "But, I am doing acts of kindness in order to atone for my many sins! Anyone would give away all he owns in order to save his own life. The halachah places no limits on how much one may spend to save his own life.

"Every mitzvah I perform is tainted with imperfection. Fortunately for me, one mitzvah does not require perfection in order to have merit. So you see, this is the only mitzvah that earns me some genuine merit."

(Mekor Chaim)

Teshuvah and Shabbos

Shabbos and teshuvah are linked. *Erev Shabbos* is an ideal time for teshuvah, as it elevates us to the holiness of Shabbos (*Ohel Shimon* 107). *Erev Shabbos* is designated for teshuvah so that we can remove the non-Jewish elements from our psyche, which are our sins, in preparation to enter Shabbos. This is because it is forbidden for a non-Jew to keep Shabbos (*Chidushei HaRim*).

If you rearrange the letters of Shabbos (*shin–beis–sav*) you get *boshes,* which means shame. Shame is the most potent tool we can use to *toshev* — return (another rearrangement of the letters of *Shabbos*). These three are interconnected. *Boshes* — shame — and teshuvah lead to Shabbos, and Shabbos is conducive to teshuvah.

Consider the following scenario: Shimon sends Reuven a large sum of money from abroad. As soon as he receives the money, Reuven contacts Shimon to thank him from the bottom of his heart for what he has done for him. A few days later, Reuven actually bumps into Shimon and once again profusely thanks him for his kindness. Even though he has already thanked him, it is proper that he do so again, now that he has met him in person.

Shabbos is an ideal opportunity to thank Hashem for the kindness He does for us all week long. Although we have surely done so throughout the course of the week, Shabbos is a time of greater intimacy when it is appropriate for us to once again thank Hashem "face to Face" as it were.

Now let us imagine that Reuven did something which greatly upset and angered the very same Shimon who had done so many favors for him. Reuven would certainly soon regret his deed and hurry to beg for forgiveness. Even after apologizing profusely on the phone, we can be sure that if he were to bump into his benefactor in person he would once again apologize for his inappropriate behavior.

This is the way we should feel every Shabbos as we prepare to meet "face to Face" with Hashem, in the more rarefied atmosphere of Shabbos. Hashem has done so much for us and during the course of the week we have angered Him numerous times. This is the shame of *Erev Shabbos* that results in teshuvah and ultimately in the level of Shabbos holiness. (*Dibros Tzvi, Parshas Devarim*)

Collective Teshuvah

We know that the entire Jewish people are linked to and have a collective responsibility for one another. From the taking of the *esrog, lulav, hadassim,* and *aravos* in one bunch, we learn that it is necessary for all the elements of our nation to join together. It is incumbent upon the righteous to associate with the simpler people and to raise their level of service to Hashem. It is imperative that each of us choose a Rav and acquire a friend, for they will help advise us how to save ourself from sin and work on self-improvement. (*Mishneh Halachos of Rabbeinu Yonah* 89)

> *Rav Meir lived near some gangsters who persecuted him terribly. In his great distress he prayed that they die, until his wife Bruriah asked, "Why do you pray for their death? Is it because of the verse saying, 'Let the sinners [chataim] cease'? Does the pasuk say 'sinners,' however? No! It says 'sins'! This can be proved by the end of the pasuk which states,*

'And sinners will be no more.' Pray rather that they repent and do teshuvah, for then there will be no more sinners." Rabbi Meir prayed that they repent and indeed, the gangsters did teshuvah.

(Berachos 10)

When the same thing happened to Abba Chilkiya, son of Choni Ha'maagal, he prayed that the wicked ones die, but his wife prayed that they repent. Her prayer was accepted — and they repented.

(Taanis)

Criminals lived in Rav Zeira's neighborhood. Rav Zeira used to daven on their behalf and tried to draw them closer to their Heavenly Father, even though the other Sages looked askance on this. When Rav Zeira died, the criminals said, "Up to now, Rav Zeira used to pray for us when we sinned. Now that he is gone, who will daven for us?" They examined their souls and did teshuvah.

(Sanhedrin)

The Yismach Moshe once repeated to his grandson the Yetev Lev of Satmar a conversation that had taken place in Heaven between Rashi and Reb Itzik'l of Druhbitz.

Rashi asked Reb Itzik'l what special merit his son, Reb Michel the Maggid of Zlotchov, possessed that his arrival was so celebrated. "Why did he deserve such a tumult in Heaven? What had he done to earn the great honor he received in the Heavenly Court?"

"My son studied Torah purely for its own sake," replied the father.

"That is not enough of a reason," insisted Rashi.

"My son mortified himself with much fasting. Perhaps that is his merit," suggested Reb Itzik'l.

"That is not enough merit, to warrant such an extraordinary reception," replied Rashi.

"He gave a lot of money to the poor. My son was constantly helping others. Doing chessed, might that be his merit?"

Rashi was not satisfied with that either. He asked Reb Itzik'l to think of something greater. Finally the latter said, "Reb Michel, my son, caused many to do teshuvah."

"Aha! That is his merit," exclaimed Rashi. "That is reason enough to warrant the huge fanfare and reception he was given here in Heaven."

(*Those Who Returned*, pg. 221–222)

INSPIRATION

After *Shemoneh Esrei* we beg, "Erase and remove our sins and transgressions from before Your eyes." This is puzzling for have we not already davened for forgiveness in the blessing *Selach Lanu*? The Chofetz Chaim explains that first we beg for forgiveness for sins we committed ourselves; later, we ask for forgiveness for the sins of other Jews for which we are responsible, because of the principle of solidarity.

The *Midrash* cites the parable of a province that was delinquent in paying its taxes, until the king marched towards it to settled accounts with its citizens.

> *When the king was ten miles from the border, the governors of the province came out to welcome him. In recognition of this gesture, the king declared that he would wipe out a third of the province's debt. When the king advanced to within five miles of the border, all the minor officials of the province came out to greet him. In recognition of this, the king wiped out another third of the province's debt.*
>
> *When the king finally crossed the border into the province, he was greeted by the entire population, whereupon he wiped out the entire debt, telling them, "Whatever has been until now is water under the bridge. Let us begin a new accounting starting today."*

Similarly, Hashem announced to us that He is coming to settle accounts with us for our actions over the past year. On *Erev Rosh Ha'shanah* the tzaddikim fast, and in that merit Hashem forgives a third of our sins. Many fast at least one day during the Ten Days of Repentance, and in that merit Hashem forgives another third of our sins.

Finally on *Yom Kippur* everyone — young and old, men and women, healthy and less so — fasts the entire night and day, and Hashem wipes away the rest of our sins. That is why the Torah calls *Succos* "*Ha'yom Ha'rishon*," the First Day, meaning that it is the first day of our fresh account with Hashem.

Based on these *midrashim* and other sources, the Satmar Rebbe taught that atonement is accomplished when the nation comes to serve Hashem *collectively* and to beg Him for forgiveness. If we wish our teshuvah to be effective, it is necessary to inspire others to join us in our efforts. Each one must reach out to others and attempt to influence them in positive ways. (Rav Yoel Teitelbaum)

The righteous attempt to reach out to others, encouraging them to do teshuvah even after they leave this world.

> *Two Jews left home on an extended business trip to distant Russia. The years passed and the two were very successful in their business endeavors. Unfortunately living among non-Jews, with no contact with their coreligionists, they slowly abandoned mitzvah observance.*
>
> *Returning home, they stopped in a village at the home of a non-Jew. He greeted them warmly, serving them a cup of hot tea. They requested a meat meal and promised that they would pay whatever it cost. He explained that he only had non-kosher meat.*
>
> *"That's fine," they replied. "We aren't fussy."*
>
> *Their host replied that it would take a while to prepare the meal. He returned a short while later with an axe in his hand. "Get ready to die!" he growled.*
>
> *The two begged for mercy to no avail.*
>
> *"It's your hard luck that you knocked on my door. I am a thief and murderer." He locked them into a*

room, from which they heard him sharpening his axe. The two suddenly felt immense remorse, and repented for all of their misdeeds. They said all the prayers they remembered, praying as they never had before, with heartrending sobs.

After some time, the door opened again. The man who opened the door was hardly recognizable. The wicked expression on his face was gone. It its place was a gentle smile

"You are free to leave," he said. "I never intended to harm you. I am far from being a murderer. Now I can explain why I frightened you as I did. Many years ago, a holy Jew passed through this village and stayed at my home. He fell ill here and passed away in this very room. Before his demise, he blessed me with a long life and made a request, 'When Jews pass through, please be welcoming. But if one of them wants nonkosher meat, threaten to kill him. Don't harm him. Just threaten him.'

"When the Jew passed away, his family buried him nearby. I closed this room after his death and only open it for Jews desiring to pray, and now for you." The Jews trembled uncontrollably as they listened to the story. After making inquiries, they discovered who the tzaddik was and where he was buried. They made their way to the Baal Ha'tanya's gravesite in Haditch, where they spent a long time praying, crying, and doing true teshuvah.

> ### Inspiration
>
> Moshe Rabbeinu was distressed that he did not participate in the donations to the *Mishkan*. Hashem comforted him by saying that his words were more precious than a tangible contribution to the *Mishkan*. (*Yalkut Shemoni, Remez* 428) Why didn't Hashem make reference to the fact that the donations were meant to be atonement for the sin of the Golden Calf, in which Moshe had not participated? Hashem knew that Moshe was troubled by being denied access to the chamber where penitents stand, which is not accessible to the righteous. In truth there was no reason to be distressed about being unable to enter this chamber in Heaven, for Moshe was responsible for bringing the Jewish people to do teshuvah and the person who enables others to do a mitzvah is greater than the person who does it. (*Bava Basra* 9:1) What Hashem was telling Moshe Rabbeinu was that Moshe's words, which inspired the Jewish people to repent, were more meritorious that each Jew's individual repentance.
>
> (Chasam Sofer on *Torah Vayikra* 1:1)

Rav Mendel of Riminov would lead the Selichos *prayer Erev Rosh Ha'shanah. When he reached the words, "If truly all have returned, calling out with heart and soul," he would pause before continuing. Year after year he would stop and wait. Many thought that he was lost in meditation, but his* disciples, the Rebbe of Ropshitz, the Bnei Yissoschar, and others, testified that he would not continue until all present were roused to repent.

(*Mi'giborei Ha'chassidus* 17)

Rav Feivish of Zebarosh once poured out his heart to the Rebbe Reb Mendel. He was eighty-four years old and still felt that he was far from complete teshuvah. His Rebbe replied, "We are in the same position. Let us bless one another that we merit doing teshuvah."

(ibid. 18)

Teshuvah in Tanach

After Adam and Chavah ate from the *Eitz Ha'daas* they hid, realizing they had done wrong. When Hashem called out to Adam, asking, "Where are you?" (*Bereishis* 3:9), Hashem's intention was to give Adam an opportunity to admit what he had done wrong (Rashi, Radak), thus initiating the teshuvah process, which he would then continue for the rest of his life.

Adam committed a single sin for which he was banished from *Gan Eden*. Death was decreed for him and all future generations, the earth was cursed to produce thorns and thistles, and man was cursed to earn his sustenance by the sweat of his brow. Yet at this terrible moment, Adam is informed, "Just as you stood before Me in judgment this day [*Rosh Ha'shanah*], so your children will stand before Me in the future and emerge blameless."

Adam's repentance included a regimen of fasting and self-torment for 130 years. During this period, he separated from his wife while girding his body with fig leaves. (*Eiruvin* 18b) The Patriarchs and Dovid Ha'melech reinforced his teshuvah, but only with the coming of *Moshiach* will his sin be fully atoned for. (*Midrash Rabbah*)

After killing Hevel, Kayin was sent into permanent exile, forced to wander forever. When Adam asked his son for the details of the punishment for the murder of his brother, Kayin told him, "I did teshuvah, and I was reconciled to the *Ribono Shel Olam*." Adam cried out in amazement, "Such is the power of teshuvah and I never knew it!" (*Bereishis Rabbah* 22:28; *Vayikra Rabbah* 10:5)

Considering that Adam spent 130 years in the most intense forms of teshuvah after his sin, how could he have declared that he was unfamiliar with the power of teshuvah (*Eiruvin* 18b)? Presumably, Adam was familiar only with complete teshuvah as described by the Rambam, where a person finds himself in exactly the same type of circumstances that led him to sin previously, with his desire for the sin unabated, and yet he does not sin.

Kayin revealed to his father the possibility of partial teshuvah and that is why Kayin uses the word "compromise" to describe his teshuvah (*Shemen Ha'tov*). Kayin said to Hashem, "My sin is too heavy to bear." How could Kayin complain about the severity of his punishment when he had perpetrated the first murder in the world? Kayin actually was claiming that being forced to wander would make his sin too great to bear, for without a measure of serenity he could not do proper teshuvah, and if he didn't repent then his sin would indeed be too great to bear. (*Emes Mi'kotzk Titzmach* 59)

Both Terach and Yishmael did teshuvah and merited their place in the World to Come (*Bava Basra* 16). Although sent away from his father's house because of his innate unruliness, Yishmael repented. Yishmael is referred to as the son of Avrohom unlike Eisav, who is not referred to as the son of Yitzchok. (*Yismach Moshe*; see *Bereishis* 25:9) Yishmael had claimed that Yitzchok was not Avrohom's son, but by allowing him to go first at their father's funeral, he acknowledged that Yitzchok was, indeed, a son following his father's coffin.

Reuven repented. As our Sages say, "And Reuven returned to the pit" (*Bereishis* 37:29). Where had he been? Rabbi Elazar said he was in sackcloth and fasting (about his sin with Bilhah), which had only been a minor misstep (*Shabbos* 45). When he had a chance, he returned and checked up on Yosef in the pit. The Almighty said to him, "Never before has someone who has sinned before Me repented. You, however, have turned to Me in teshuvah first; by your life, one of your descendants will also be famous for calling for repentance." Who is he? Hoshea, who said: "Return Israel unto the Almighty, your G-d" (*Hoshea* 14:12). (*Bereishis Rabbah* 84)

The commentaries ask the obvious question: How is it that the *Midrash* praises Reuven as the first person to repent? Hadn't both Adam and Kayin already preceded Reuven in the act of repentance? The Alexander Rebbe explains the difference. Reuven's repentance was immediate and complete. The Torah testifies to Reuven's righteousness, immediately after the event, by including him in the tally of Yaakov's children (*Bereishis* 35:22). Even so, he continued to repent, thus moving into a category all his own. (*Admorei Alexander*, pg. 128–129)

The Kotzker Rebbe zeroes in on Reuven's ability to identify the sinful, subconscious motives of the brothers as an indication that his repentance was infinitely more refined than that of Adam and Kayin. Reuven's trailblazing recognition of his egotistical motives in trying to save Yosef, and his subsequent attempt to do the mitzvah with a pure and holy intention were his primary contribution to the teshuvah process. (*Ohel Torah* 18) This type of teshuvah requires a great deal more integrity.

Yehudah's teshuvah is described next. "And at that time, Yehudah went down from his brothers…. and Yehudah saw there the daughter of a certain Canaanite, whose name was Shua, and he took her in marriage" (*Bereishis* 38:1–2).

"Rabbi Shmuel bar Nachman expounds: 'For I know all the thoughts' (*Yirmiyahu* 29:11); the tribes were occupied with their grief over the sale of Yosef into *Mitzrayim*. Yosef was occupied with his sackcloth and fasting. Reuven was occupied with his sackcloth and fasting. Where was Yehudah? He was busy taking a wife. And what was Hashem doing? Hashem was busy creating the light of *Moshiach*." (*Bereishis Rabbah* 85:3)

The Kotzker Rebbe explains: "When Yehudah saw what had happened, that he had the full lion's share of responsibility because of his suggestion to sell Yosef, his heart grew weak inside him and a great and bitter remorse overcame him, until his very existence was actually nullified. He judged himself severely and came to the decisive conclusion that all the spiritual merits and growth he had amassed since his birth had been utterly destroyed. His soul nearly left him from the vast impact of this bitter realization, until he finally grew calm, and fortified his spirit once more; he decided to begin to practice the Torah anew, from the very beginning, and to prepare his heart from then on to serve Hashem, like a newborn infant (since he had lost all his spiritual merits and accomplishments). So he began his service of Hashem anew, from the very first mitzvah in the Torah: "Be fruitful and multiply" (*Bereishis* 1:28). This thought was so dear to Hashem, the One Who "knows all thoughts" and scrutinizes the inner hearts of men, that He created the light of *Moshiach* from the seed of Yehudah." (*Lahavos Kodesh* 30:1)

The children of Korach were saved from destruction by their teshuvah. Even though they ostensibly supported their father, they repented in their hearts and they were placed in a protected place in *Gehinnom*, where they were shielded from the fierce punishments. (Rashi)

Rachav was ten years old when she began her sinful career. For forty years she lived a life of immorality. When she repented, she rose to a very high spiritual level. The Torah testifies that she merited *ruach ha'kodesh* (see Rashi in *Yehoshua* 2:16). She was deemed worthy to marry Yehoshua and to have eight prophets descend from her. Such is the power of teshuvah.

Nineveh was another Sodom. When Yonah rebuked the citizens of that city, the king arose from his throne, removed his royal robes, donned sackcloth, and sat in the dust. Man and animals abstained from food and called out to Hashem in repentance. Thus were they saved. (See *Sefer Yonah*)

Dovid Ha'melech shed bitter tears for twenty-two years, eating only bread dipped in ashes to atone for his flawed judgment in the incident with Bathsheva (*Tehillim* 102; *Tanna De'bei Eliyahu*). All his trials and tribulations with Avshalom and Shimi were lovingly accepted so that he might atone for not having fully passed that fateful test. The *Zohar* points out that if Dovid had lived another thirty years, enabling him to continue his teshuvah regimen, he would have been able to rectify Adam's sin. (*Zohar, Rus*)

Achav, King of Israel, committed many transgressions: he robbed, he lusted, and he killed, but afterwards he did teshuvah and he called Yehoshafat, king of Yehudah, who flogged him three times a day. He fasted and davened early and late to Hashem and did not revert to his evil practices. It took great courage on his part to submit to a public flogging. (*Oros Ha'chaim* 81) Because his repentance was genuine, Hashem declared it accepted. As it is written (*Melachim I* 21:29): "Do you see that Achav has humbled himself before Me? Because he has humbled himself before Me, I will not bring the evil in his days." (*Pirkei De'Rebbi Eliezer*)

Yechaniah was so wicked that Hashem said of him: "If Yechanyah the son of Yeoyakim, king of Yehudah, were the signet ring on My Right Hand [which is never removed], I would cast him aside" (*Yirmiyahu* 22:24). And Yirmiyahu declared in Hashem's Name that Yechanyah would die childless, without an heir to sit on the throne of Yehudah (*Yirmiyahu* 22:30). Yet at one point, Yechonya restrained from sinning, despite temptation. Hashem saw his teshuvah and annulled the vow that he would die childless. After he did teshuvah, Hashem referred to him as His "signet ring." (*Hilchos Teshuvah* 7:6) His teshuvah altered his life and that of his descendants, and changed the course of Jewish history. His great-grandson, the tzaddik, Zerubavel ruled over Yehudah when the exiles returned. (Radak, ibid.)

King Menashe was sinful beyond description. He reigned for fifty-five years and was notorious for having placed an idol in the Temple (*Melachim II* 21). The *Gemara* discusses the fact that after twenty-two years of wickedness, he was dragged off to Babylon, tortured, and he repented. The verse in *Divrei Ha'yamim II* (33) states with regard to this: "*Va-ye'chateir lo,*" that Hashem created a subterfuge for him. After suggesting a more plausible alternative text, the *Gemara* concludes that the strange choice of language in the verse indicates that, according to the strict law, Menashe was not worthy of forgiveness, yet out of the goodness of His Heart, Hashem, as it were, allowed him to repent "through the back door." Thus, Menashe, who caused others to sin and thus was not deserving of forgiveness (see Rambam as cited above), was granted a Divine pardon as a *chessed* and so that future penitents would learn from his experience. (*Devarim Rabbah* 2:13) All who say that Menashe has no share in the World to Come weaken the hands of penitents, for a *Tanna* taught in the presence of Rabbi Yochanan: "Menashe repented for thirty-three years, and the Holy One Blessed be He accepted Him" (*Sanhedrin* 103a).

Even if one has come to a point where a he doesn't have a single mitzvah or good deed to plead for him, in which case justice does not offer any chance for his repentance to be accepted, he can still ask Hashem in His boundless *chessed* to accept him, beyond the strictures of justice. In the Penitent's Prayer of Rabbeinu Yonah, man calls out to Hashem, "And if because of my great, overwhelming sin, I have no advocate, not even one — You dig a tunnel for me under Your Throne and accept my repentance, that I may not leave Your presence empty-handed. (*Yesod Ha'teshuvah*)

Barriers to Repentance

There are a number of transgressions that raise barriers, that make it really hard to return to Hashem, for they distance Divine assistance from us. Our *yetzer tov* may not be strong enough to carry us through. Such actions should be avoided at all costs. These transgressions are divided into five groups, some more severe than others. The Rambam, in *Hilchos Teshuvah*, lists these sins. He stresses that, even so, nothing stands in the way of repentance:

1) "There are twenty-four things for which repentance cannot be [readily] done. Four of these are very great sins, and if one commits any of them, God will not accept one's repentance, due to the gravity of the sin. These four are as follows:

   (a) "Causing many others to sin, including preventing them from fulfilling a mitzvah." For example, a group of people have decided to give charity to a worthy cause, and someone persuades them not to do so.

(b) "Influencing a virtuous person to do evil." An example might be introducing someone to Internet use.

(c) "Not preventing one's child from entering a bad culture. Since one's child is in one's charge, not trying to prevent this would be tantamount to causing him to sin. Included in this category is not trying to prevent another person from doing wrong, instead leaving him to his failings."

(d) "One who says 'I will sin, then repent; I will sin, then repent' is not allowed to repent" (*Yoma* 85b). If a person continues to sin, not as a result of passion, intending afterwards to erase all his sins through teshuvah, Hashem withholds from his the opportunity of repenting.

A Jew once asked Rav Asher of Stolin, "Is it possible to do teshuvah for a sin which the Torah teaches defies repentance?"

Rav Asher replied, "What business is it of yours whether the teshuvah will help or not? You must do what is incumbent upon you. Are you afraid that you will have no Olam Ha'ba? In answer to this, our Sages taught that 'one hour of teshuvah and good deeds in This World is better than all of Olam Ha'ba' "

(*Those Who Returned*, pg. 222)

> ### Food For Thought
>
> "Two things are so near and yet so far, so far yet so near. Repentance is so near, yet so far; so far, but yet so near to you. Death is so near to you, yet so far; so far, but yet so near."
>
> *(Koheles Rabbah 8)*

Just before he left to get married, a talmid from Ponovezh Yeshivah commented that he had learned three things that are really four things: "I learned that there is a Creator; I learned that there is reward and punishment; I learned that I will die. And the fourth thing I learned was that, while initially I thought that I knew and understood these truths, after hearing the Mashgiach [Rav Yechezkel Levenstein] speak on these topics, it is clear to me now that previously I just thought I knew and understood them."

(Reb Chatzkel, pg. 205)

2) "There are five sins which lock the Gates of Repentance." The following sins often stem from personality disorders, which can create mental and emotional states that make a person so self-satisfied that repenting becomes difficult.

(a) "Disassociating oneself from the community. For when such a person repents, he won't be associated with the community or with the merit of the community's repentance" (Rabbeinu Yonah, *Shaarei Teshuvah* 3) explains that when a community gathers to initiate some good actions and someone chooses not to join them, this person is debasing the service of Hashem. He is also held responsible for cooling the ardor of those who are enthusiastic in their performance of mitzvos.

The Ohr Yechezkel writes that the Rambam is referring to people who are observant, but who lag behind their contemporaries who seek greater spiritual heights. Everyone is part of a community. If one chooses not to join the community in its spiritual endeavors, then he has disassociated himself from the community.

(b) "Arguing with the words of the Sages. For such arguing causes one to disassociate, and then one won't know [how to reach] the Gates of Repentance." This means that when it conflicts with his own opinions, he does not accept *daas Torah*.

(c) "Mocking the mitzvos. Doing so makes them as nothing, so that the person won't fulfill them. Yet if he doesn't fulfill them, how else will he accrue merits?!"

Those who mock the mitzvos remain unmoved even by open miracles. The Ohr Yahel asks why Moshe didn't at once respond to Korach's challenge by setting up the rods and letting the rod of Aharon blossom so that Korach's argument would immediately be refuted. He answers that Moshe could not immediately provide this evidence, which would have put an end to the rebellion, because while under the influence of mockery, they would have remained unconvinced! Only after witnessing the dramatic punishment of Korach and his cohorts could they assimilate the evidence. (*Parshas Korach*)

(d) "Disgracing one's rabbis. For this causes one to be repelled and loathed, like Gehazi. When one is bothered, it will transpire that he will not find a teacher to teach him the proper way."

Rabbeinu Yonah writes that whoever disgraces a Torah scholar has no portion in the World to Come.

(e) "Hating rebuke. For this obstructs repentance." Rebuke leads to repentance. When a person needs to be awakened, he cannot do so himself. It is easier for someone else to awaken him. Only if someone rebukes him does the person stand a chance of doing teshuvah. (*Ohr Yechezkel*)

One who hates rebuke will not be affected by it and will continue in his wicked ways, which in his opinion are fine.

Food For Thought

Through one mocking gesture, one can flatten tall edifices of spiritual ferver. When the heart is aroused, one critical remark can douse the fire, not because the idea is weak or not well absorbed, but because of the power of mockery to destroy fear of G-d.

(*Mesilas Yesharim* 5)

3) "There are five sins for which there is no complete repentance, because one doesn't know against whom exactly one had sinned, in order to pay him back and ask for forgiveness. These sins are:

(a) "Cursing a group of people, not a particular person, for one can ask an individual for forgiveness."

(b) "Abetting with a thief. Because one doesn't know to whom the stolen articles belong. The thief steals from many people, bringing all the stolen goods to one place. Furthermore, this help encourages the thief to steal; therefore, one is causing him to sin."

(c) "Finding a lost article, but not searching for its owner. When one eventually repents, one will not know to whom to return it."

(d) "Making use of charity money that has been set aside for poor people, orphans, and widows. Such people are miserable, moving from town to town, and not well known. Anybody who uses their charity money won't know to whom to pay it back."

(e) "Accepting a bribe in judgment. One who does so will not feel as though his judgment is affected [For 'bribes blind (even) the wise.'] and so will not correct this, for an inevitable reaction is uncontrollable. Furthermore, one is causing the briber to sin."

4) "There are five sins for which one [probably] won't repent, because in most people's opinions these are minor and not even considered as sins." A person does not take these sins seriously and they become deeply ingrained in his psyche:

(a) "Eating a meal where one's host will be left with insufficient food for his next meal; this is also akin to theft. One who does this will not consider it a sin, and will try to justify it by saying that he had permission to eat."

(b) "Using the collateral of a loan given to a poor person, such as his shovel. One who acts in this way will think that the poor person isn't lacking the item and will not count it as theft." The Kav Ha'yashar adds that this includes speaking harshly to a poor man, knowing that he will not respond. Hashem will intervene to protect the interests of the poor person.

Everyone in Jerusalem knew old Berel Zlodowitz. Poor old Berel, a lonely soul who lived in an old-age home in one of the new neighborhoods outside the city walls. It was rumored that back in Russia, before the Revolution, Berel had been a wealthy man, with a chain of textile factories in the Minsk area and philanthropic projects all over the world. Some said that he had built the very institution whose charity now housed and fed him.

If these rumors were true, nothing remained of his former glory. Berel was a shadow of a man, destitute, friendless, and eccentric. He had a habit of begging cigarettes, asking every passerby, "Please, could I have a cigarette?" No one ever saw him smoke these cigarettes, nor could he possibly have smoked them all — he must have begged a hundred cigarettes each day.

But one day, old Berel underwent a dramatic transformation. There was a smile in his eyes, a lightness in his step; even his bent old back seemed to have somewhat straightened. He began speaking to people and even stopped begging cigarettes. Suddenly he was revealed as a lively old man, with a lucid mind and a healthy spirit.

One man knew the story behind Berel's metamorphosis: Rabbi Yechiel Michel Tukochinsky, who headed the Eitz Chayim institutions in Jerusalem, which included the old-age home where Berel resided. Only years later, after Berel had passed on to his eternal rest, did Rabbi Tukochinsky reveal what he knew about Berel Zlodowitz.

Reb Yechiel's acquaintance with Berel went back many years. They had met when Reb Yechiel was in Minsk raising funds for his charitable works. Berel had welcomed Reb Yechiel into his luxurious office, and agreed to sponsor the building and maintenance of a home for the old and destitute of Jerusalem. Berel had continued to correspond with Reb Yechiel and to send his annual pledge, until this was disrupted by the outbreak of World War I.

The next time Reb Yechiel saw him, Berel was a penniless refugee knocking on his door in Jerusalem. Needless to say, the former patron was given a room at the old-age home, and all his needs were provided for as best as the institution was able in those lean years. Reb Yechiel would drop by each day to sit for a few minutes with Berel. His heart would ache at the sight of his old friend, whose troubles had left him broken in body and spirit.

One morning, when Reb Yechiel knocked on Berel's door, he was greeted with a broad smile — for the first time in twenty years. "Reb Yechiel!" Berel exclaimed. "Today I have been granted a new lease on life. This is the happiest day of my life!"

"Sit down, Reb Yechiel," continued the old man, "and let me tell you a little about myself. You know what I was and what I am today, but you don't know how it happened. I do. I have only myself to blame. Hashem blessed me with wealth and good fortune and I failed to make proper use of His blessings. Yes, I gave generously to charity. Yes, my factories provided a livelihood to hundreds of Jewish families. But I was blind to the true significance of my wealth, blind to my responsibilities toward Hashem and man.

"I thought that my wealth was mine, my due for my business accumen and toil. I thought that my workers owed me their lives for the few pennies I gave them to feed their families. I was a tyrant who used his power to crush those who failed to please him. If a worker was late to work or lax in fulfilling my expectations of him, I lashed out at him, deducted money from his wages, and threatened to fire him — a threat I often carried out — for there was no shortage of able-bodied men crowding the cities and begging for work. I shudder to think of how many lives I destroyed with my heartlessness. True, almost all the factories in Russia operated in this way, but does that excuse my behavior?

"One incident would haunt me for many years to come. A worker had come to work ten minutes late. I summoned him to my office. When the man mumbled something about a sick wife, I said coldly, 'So your wife is sick. What concern is that of mine?' I then sent him back to work after deducting half a day's pay, as clearly stipulated in the rules posted on the factory gate.

"In my mind, this incident marks the turning point of my life. Shortly thereafter, the Bolsheviks stripped me of all my possessions. Somehow, I managed to avoid arrest when the industrialists of Minsk were rounded up. I escaped across the border into Poland and made my way to Jerusalem.

"Here I found shelter and respite, but no tranquility. I was haunted — not by memories of my lost wealth, but by the realization of the type of person it had made me. I kept thinking of the worker who had tended all night to his sick wife, cowering before me in my office, pleading for his job. How did it feel to be at the mercy of another human being, to be humiliated by his callous indifference to your fate? I had to know. I felt that until I had experienced what I had made that man experience, I would not find atonement for my soul.

"So I decided to become a beggar. I didn't want to collect money — I was loathe to handle the vile stuff — and all my needs were generously provided *by your institution. So I begged cigarettes. For hours each day I stood on the street, asking passersby for cigarettes. But everyone treated me kindly, perhaps because they had heard of who I had been or out of pity for an old man somewhat soft in the head.*

"This morning, I approached an elegantly-dressed gentleman and asked for a cigarette. The man eyed me coldly and said, 'So you want a cigarette. What concern is that of mine?' His words, and especially the tone in which they were said, cut to the quick of my soul. Never had I been so humiliated. For a moment, I felt that I was nothing, that my existence was utterly without worth. And then an icy shudder passed through me. Why, these were exactly the words I had said to that worker in my factory more than twenty years ago! Suddenly I was filled with an incredible joy. The circle had been closed. Now I can die in peace, knowing that Hashem has accepted my repentance...."

(c) "Gazing at *arayos*. One who does this will think of it as nothing, because he did not touch the person. He does not know that gazing is a great sin and leads to sin. As it is written, '... and that you do not stray after your heart and after your own eyes'" (*Bamidbar* 15).

(d) "One who revels in someone else's degradation will not consider this a sin. Because the person was not standing there and was not shamed or embarrassed. He is merely comparing that person's deeds to his own, [thinking] that he will be more respected and the other person will be shamed."

(e) "One who suspects upright people [of sinning] will not consider this a sin. Because he will think he is causing no damage by "just" being suspicious. He does not know that it is a great sin to consider upright people who to be sinners."

5) "There are five sins to which people who commit them are drawn, finding it difficult to desist. Therefore, one has to be careful to avoid them, for they all are extremely bad. These sins include slander, tale-bearing, and anger." Even family members fear a person of this temperament, who ignores the cries of the poor, does not judge properly, curses continuously, readily humiliates others, but is not ashamed of anything he does, who takes revenge and is always ready for a fight (*Kav Ha'yashar*). The Rambam continues to describe the remaining two sins: "Having bad thoughts; this person gives bad advice to others and thinks nothing of bringing conflict on himself and others. He helps the wicked, never rebuking them, and is happy to see someone suffering. The last category is becoming friends with a wicked person, because one will learn from his actions and will become wicked. Shlomo Ha'melech said, 'A companion of fools shall suffer harm' [*Mishlei* 13]. It has already been explained in the Laws of Temperaments what one has to accustom oneself to. How much more so a penitent [has to accustom himself to these things]."

6) "None of these sins completely prevents repentance, though they may inhibit it. If somebody repented for having

committed one of these sins, his repentance is accepted, and he will get a share in the World to Come."

It was only hours before Yom Kippur *when Rebbe Leib Sarah's found himself some distance from his intended destination. But he was relieved to learn that in this village, too, there would be a minyan with which to pray — eight villagers and two men who lived in the nearby forest.*

In preparation for the holy day, Reb Leib immersed himself in the river that ran by the village. He ate the meal that precedes the fast, and hastened to the little wooden shul. There he settled down to recite the various private devotions with which he was accustomed to inaugurate the Day of Atonement.

One by one, the eight villagers arrived to hear Kol Nidrei. Together with Reb Leib there were now nine. But there was no minyan, for the two Jewish foresters had been imprisoned on some malicious libel.

"Perhaps we could find just one more Jew living around these parts?" asked Reb Leib.

"No," the villagers all assured him. "There's only us."

"Perhaps," he persisted, "there lives here some Jew, an apostate, who deserted the faith of his fathers?"

The villagers were shocked to hear such an odd question from the stranger. They looked at him quizzically.

"The doors of repentance are not locked even in the face of an apostate," Reb Leib continued. "I have heard from my teachers that even when stirs the

ashes with a poker, one can ignite a spark of fire...."

"There is one apostate here," one of the villagers ventured. "He is our poritz, who owns this whole village. But he has been sunk in sin for forty years. The gentile daughter of the previous poritz fell in love with him. Her father promised him that if he became a Christian and married the girl, he would be the poritz's sole heir. He did exactly that.... They had no children, and his wife died many years ago; he now lives alone in his huge mansion. He is a cruel master, and deals especially harshly with the Jews on his land."

"Show me his mansion," said Reb Leib.

They took him there. He quickly removed his tallis, and strode hurriedly up to the mansion, with his white yarmulke on his head and his white kittel billowing in the wind. He knocked on the heavy door, opened it without waiting for a response, and found himself confronting the poritz. For a few long, long moments they stood in silence face to face, the tzaddik and the apostate. The man's first thought was to summon one of his henchmen to seize the uninvited intruder and hurl him into the dungeon. But the luminous countenance and the loving, penetrating eyes of the tzaddik softened his heart.

"My name is Leib Sarah's," began the visitor. "It was my privilege to know Rabbi Yisrael, the Baal Shem Tov. From his mouth I once heard that every Jew should utter the sort of prayer that was first said by Dovid Ha'melech: 'Save me, O Lord, from blood-guilt.' But the word used for 'blood' [damim] can also be translated as 'money.' So my teacher expounded the verse as follows: 'Save me, so that I should never regard money as my lord....'

"My mother, whose name was Sarah, was a holy woman. The son of one of the local gentry took it into his head to marry her, and promised her wealth and status if she would agree. To save herself from that villain, she quickly married an elderly, impoverished melamed. You did not have the good fortune to withstand the test; for silver and gold you were willing to forsake your faith. Realize, though, that there is nothing that can stand in the way of repentance. Moreover, there are those who in one hour earn their portion in the World to Come. Now is that hour! Today is Erev Yom Kippur. The sun will soon set. The Jews who live in your village are short one man to make up a minyan. Come along now with me, and be the tenth man. For the Torah tells us: 'The tenth shall be holy unto G-d.' "

"By the sanction of the Almighty, and by the sanction of the congregation, we declare it permissible to pray together with those who have sinned..." The poritz paled at the words spoken by this white-clothed man with the noble face. Meanwhile, down the road, the eight villagers waited in shul, huddled together in frozen dread. Who could tell what calamity this odd stranger was about to bring down on their heads?

The door burst open, and in rushed Reb Leib, followed closely by the poritz. The latter's gaze was downcast, and his eyelashes were heavy with tears. At a sign from Reb Leib, one of the villagers handed the man a tallis. He enveloped himself in it, covering his head and face entirely. Reb Leib now stepped forward to the Holy Ark, and took out two scrolls of the Torah. One he gave to the oldest villager present, and the other — to the poritz. Between them at the bimah *stood Reb Leib, and he began to solemnly chant the traditional opening lines of the* Kol Nidrei *prayer:* "By the sanction of the Almighty, and by the sanction of the congregation ... we declare it permissible to pray together with those who have sinned...."

A deep sigh broke forth from the depths of the broken man's heart. No one there could stand unmoved, and they all wept with him. Throughout all the prayers of the evening, and from dawn of the next day right until nightfall, the poritz stood in prayer, humbled and contrite. And as his sobs shook his whole body, when he recited the confession, the other nine shuddered with him.

At the culmination of the Neilah *service, when the congregation was about to shout together the words "Shema Yisrael," the poritz leaned forward until his head was deep inside the Holy Ark, embraced the Torah scrolls that stood there, and in a mighty voice that petrified those present cried out:* "Shema Yisrael, *the Lord our G-d, the Lord is One!" He then stood up straight, and began to declare with all his might: "The Lord is G-d!" With each repetition his voice grew louder. Finally, as he cried it out for the seventh time, his soul flew from his body.*

That same night, they brought the remains of the poritz to burial. Reb Leib himself took part in the purification and preparation of the body for burial. For the rest of his life he observed the yahrzeit *of this penitent every* Yom Kippur, *by saying* Kaddish *for the elevation of his soul.*

(Mipi Chassidim)

Afterword

"Teshuvah is like the sea, which is never barred, so that whoever desires to bathe in it can do so whenever he desires."

Midrash Tehillim 65:4

Certainly this fact is a true cause for celebration. How grateful we ought to be for Hashem's kindness in making teshuvah always accessible to us. How marvelous to be able to totally submerge ourselves in the healing waters of repentance; see our sins washed away; and experience the joys of a fresh, new beginning. The person who emerges after teshuvah's cleansing is very different from the person he was before teshuvah.

We can demonstrate our appreciation for this opportunity to repair all the breaches in our relationship with Hashem by consistently turning to Him in repentance. This *sefer* has presented various facets of teshuvah. It has sought to serve as a guide through the teshuvah process, as it helps draw us closer to Hashem. Ultimately teshuvah must be developed